"Well-known author Frank Thielman succinctly unfolds the central plot of the whole Bible. He does not just retell the story; he explains it. And he does not merely explain it; he applies it so we can see the Bible's point right now: 'This is the great hope of the follower of Jesus in the midst of life's many present difficulties.' To grasp that hope, read this book! It is a delightful, deeply biblical, clear, and compelling narration and proclamation of God's antidote to our world's painfully visible breakdown. There's a new world order taking shape. This book equips and invites the reader to join in right now."

Robert W. Yarbrough, Professor of New Testament, Covenant Theological Seminary

"Careful study of the Scriptures is vital for Christian growth, and study of small portions of text pays great dividends. But if we cannot put those smaller bits into the larger storyline of Scripture, we can miss the forest for the trees. Frank Thielman provides a well-written and accurate description of that forest, the big picture of what God is doing in redemptive history."

Douglas J. Moo, Kenneth T. Wessner Professor of New Testament, Wheaton College; Chair, Committee on Bible Translation (NIV); author, *The Epistle to the Romans* and *An Introduction to the New Testament*

"In this concise study, Frank Thielman helpfully explains how the Bible is framed by two acts of divine creation that are intimately connected. Moving judiciously from Genesis to Revelation, he shows how God's blueprint of salvation for a world gone awry centers on Jesus Christ, the servant-king, who establishes God's new society of love, justice, kindness, and peace in anticipation of a glorious new creation. For anyone wishing to understand better the overarching story of God's plan for the whole creation, this is an excellent introduction."

T. Desmond Alexander, Senior Lecturer in Biblical Studies and Director of Postgraduate Studies, Union Theological College; author, *The City of God and the Goal of Creation* and *From Eden to the New Jerusalem*

"A succinct and brilliant study of the interlacing tapestry of biblical theology. Frank Thielman is the kind of scholar we need more of—he writes with clarity and devotion and always brings us closer to Christ."

Timothy George, Distinguished Professor of Divinity, Beeson Divinity School, Samford University

"Frank Thielman proves to be the ideal guide for a tour of the Bible. Taking *new creation* as an organizing theme, he directs attention to the critical junctures in the biblical story. Without getting bogged down in excessive detail, he uses his expert knowledge to spotlight the big structure that holds the Bible together. The result is a book that is as easy to read as it is illuminating. Readers will come away with a deeper love of God and a greater sense of gratitude for his salvation."

Sigurd Grindheim, Professor, Western Norway University of Applied Sciences

"Frank Thielman's *The New Creation and the Storyline of Scripture* is a remarkable achievement. He has distilled the vast reservoir of information provided in the Bible on the subject to its essential elements, while packing his 120-page presentation with a remarkable amount of Scripture. This handy volume challenges Christ followers to live as transformed creations in this age and heightens our anticipation of life with God in the world to come."

Daniel I. Block, Gunther H. Knoedler Professor Emeritus of Old Testament, Wheaton College; author, *The Triumph of Grace* and *For the Glory of God*

The New Creation and the Storyline of Scripture

The New Creation and the Storyline of Scripture

Frank Thielman

CROSSWAY®

WHEATON, ILLINOIS

Cover design: Jordan Singer

First printing 2021

Printed in the United States of America

Trade paperback ISBN: 978-1-4335-5955-6
ePub ISBN: 978-1-4335-5958-7
PDF ISBN: 978-1-4335-5956-3
Mobipocket ISBN: 978-1-4335-5957-0

Library of Congress Cataloging-in-Publication Data

Names: Thielman, Frank, author.
Title: The new creation and the storyline of Scripture / Frank Thielman.
Description: Wheaton, Illinois : Crossway, [2021] | Series: Short studies in biblical theology | Includes bibliographical references and index.
Identifiers: LCCN 2020001164 | ISBN 9781433559556 (trade paperback) | ISBN 9781433559563 (pdf) | ISBN 9781433559570 (mobi) | ISBN 9781433559587 (epub)
Subjects: LCSH: Creation—Biblical teaching | Bible. New Testament—Criticism, interpretation, etc. | Bible. New Testament—Introductions.
Classification: LCC BS651 .T4825 2021 | DDC 231.7/6—dc23
LC record available at https://lccn.loc.gov/2020001164

Crossway is a publishing ministry of Good News Publishers.

BP   30 29 28 27 26 25 24 23 22 21
15 14 13 12 11 10 9 8 7 6 5 4 3 2 1

For Isaiah James Thielman
and for his wonderful parents, Jonathan and Emily

Contents

Series Preface

Most of us tend to approach the Bible early on in our Christian lives as a vast, cavernous, and largely impenetrable book. We read the text piecemeal, finding golden nuggets of inspiration here and there, but remain unable to plug any given text meaningfully into the overarching storyline. Yet one of the great advances in evangelical biblical scholarship over the past few generations has been the recovery of biblical theology—that is, a renewed appreciation for the Bible as a theologically unified, historically rooted, progressively unfolding, and ultimately Christ-centered narrative of God's covenantal work in our world to redeem sinful humanity.

This renaissance of biblical theology is a blessing, yet little of it has been made available to the general Christian population. The purpose of Short Studies in Biblical Theology is to connect the resurgence of biblical theology at the academic level with everyday believers. Each volume is written by a capable scholar or churchman who is consciously writing in a way that requires no prerequisite theological training of the reader. Instead, any thoughtful Christian disciple can track with and benefit from these books.

Each volume in this series takes a whole-Bible theme and traces it through Scripture. In this way readers not only learn about a given theme but also are given a model for how to read the Bible as a coherent whole.

We have launched this series because we love the Bible, we love the church, and we long for the renewal of biblical theology in the academy to enliven the hearts and minds of Christ's disciples all around the world. As editors, we have found few discoveries more thrilling in life than that of seeing the whole Bible as a unified story of God's gracious acts of redemption, and indeed of seeing the whole Bible as ultimately about Jesus, as he himself testified (Luke 24:27; John 5:39).

The ultimate goal of Short Studies in Biblical Theology is to magnify the Savior and to build up his church—magnifying the Savior through showing how the whole Bible points to him and his gracious rescue of helpless sinners; and building up the church by strengthening believers in their grasp of these life-giving truths.

Dane C. Ortlund and Miles V. Van Pelt

Preface

My hope for this short book is that it serves as a basic introduction to the plotline of the Christian Scriptures. There are many interesting and valuable ways to approach the Bible. The Scripture is filled with exciting stories and heart-stirring poetry, so it is not surprising that some people turn to it for cultural enrichment. It is also a book full of historical significance, giving valuable evidence, some of it unparalleled anywhere else, for the political and cultural world of Middle Eastern antiquity. Historians find it indispensable. The Bible raises a host of moral and ethical issues, so people with questions about how life is best lived often want to know what particular passages say about this or that philosophical problem.

None of these approaches to the Bible do it a disservice, but none of them are focused on the message of the Bible itself. It is true that the Bible is a collection of texts written over a wide span of time, but it also has a basic storyline and a basic meaning. Taken together, these texts ask to be read in a particular way and claim to be saying something of great importance for all humanity and for each human individual. My hope for this book is that it functions as an introduction to this story and this message.

In describing the Bible's message, I have focused my attention on its interest in the "new creation." This is a phrase that appears only twice in the Christian Scriptures, but it summarizes the Bible's plotline neatly because it takes in the sweep of the world's history from the Bible's perspective. To call the world a "creation" assumes that it has a Creator, and to refer to a "new creation" implies that something happened to the world that makes its renewal necessary. Within its first several pages, the Bible tells its audience who this Creator is and how his creation perfectly reflected his character. It also describes how the only part of creation that God made in his image rebelled against him and set the world on a downward spiral that is vividly reflected in the suffering that now mars the existence of every human being. Because God's character is gracious and merciful, however, he did not leave his human creatures without forgiveness or hope but immediately began to work toward their rescue and the renewal of all that he had made.

This book is an introduction, so I have treated not every biblical text but eight parts of the Bible that move its storyline forward from creation to new creation in particularly long strides: Genesis 1–4, Isaiah, Matthew, Acts, Galatians, 2 Corinthians, Ephesians, and Revelation 21–22. Although I occasionally reproduce the texts I am discussing, readers will find it easier to follow the book's argument if they read it with a copy of the Bible close at hand for reference. It will also be helpful to take some time to read liberally around whatever passage is under discussion. The introductory nature of the book also means that the footnotes occasionally record my indebtedness to other interpreters, but they mainly point the reader in the direction of literature that will be helpful for further study. I have provided an alphabetical list of those works in a section at the end titled "For Further Reading." I am grateful to Miles Van Pelt, Dane Ortlund, and David Barshinger for their careful reading of this book and helpful recommendations for revision. It is a better book because of their involvement, and I deeply appreciate the time they took to help me with it.

I have dedicated this book to my sweet little grandson, Isaiah, who is so aptly named, and to his parents, Jonathan and Emily. Although Isaiah has spent a lot of time in the hospital during his first two years, he is a smiling, laughing, sociable toddler who brings joy to everyone he meets. Jonathan and Emily have simply been wonderful parents to Isaiah, and I thought constantly of their faithfulness, courage, and trust in God as I wrote on the new creation.

This book took shape during a summer that my wife, Abby, and I were able to spend with Isaiah, Jonathan, and Emily thanks to the hospitality of my brother and sister-in-law, Nathan and Margaret Thielman, and our friends Rick and Sonya Hove. I could write another book describing all that each of these wonderful friends and relatives means to me. Suffice it to say that I owe them—especially my dear wife, Abby—an enormous debt of gratitude for their Christlike example of self-giving generosity, not least in carving out time and space for me both to work on this book and to enjoy being with Isaiah.

Frank Thielman
Advent 2019

A Good World Goes Awry

The Scriptures are clear that the one God, who is himself perfectly good, created a perfectly good universe, and that the crowning achievement of his creative activity was the formation of two perfectly good human beings in his own image. The Scriptures communicate this truth in the opening paragraphs of the first book in the Bible, Genesis 1:1–2:3. Unfortunately, the Scriptures also make clear that the world did not remain the way God created it, and they tell the story of what happened to God's good world in Genesis 2:4–4:26.

A Good God and His Creation

Genesis 1:1–2:3 is an intricately crafted narrative whose form serves its message, and that message is clear. One transcendent being, God, designed the world, and his design was ordered, balanced, and good.

As students of this narrative have often observed, it is itself meticulously designed to emphasize the number seven. There are seven words in the Hebrew text of the first sentence (1:1). The narrative's climactic concluding paragraph (2:1–3) features God himself resting on the seventh day, and it expresses this act in thirty-five Hebrew words, a word count that is equal to five times seven.[1] Seven, then, is clearly the number that in some way corresponds to God.

Seven, as it turns out, is also the number that corresponds to God's creative activity, the story of which appears sandwiched between the first sentence and the last paragraph. Seven times, God's creative word ("Let there be light. . . . Let there be an expanse. . . . Let dry land appear. . . . Let the earth sprout vegetation. . . . Let there be lights. . . . Let the earth bring forth living creatures . . .") or his provision ("I have given every green plant for food") is matched with the phrase "And it was so" or, in 1:3, its equivalent (1:3, 6–7, 9, 11, 14–15, 24, 30). This pattern communicates that what God intends actually comes to pass and that both what he intends and what comes to pass in creation correspond to who he is.

Who is he? He is good, as the sevenfold repetition of the phrase "And God saw that it was good" demonstrates, especially in its more emphatic form at the end of the sixth day: "And God saw everything that he had made, and behold, it was very good" (1:4, 10, 12, 18, 21, 25, 31). The goodness of creation reflects the goodness of God.

The goodness of creation also appears in the order and balance of the creation narrative. The six days of creation are neatly ordered in two groups of three, with the first, second, and third day in each group corresponding to each other. God creates light on day one and the heavenly bodies that give light (sun, moon, and stars) on day four (1:3–5, 14–19). He creates sky and sea on day two and the animals that inhabit the sky and sea (birds and fish) on day five (1:6–8, 20–23). He creates land and plants on day three and the creatures that inhabit the land and will eat the plants (animals and human beings) on day six (1:11–13, 24–31).[2]

---

1. Nahum M. Sarna, *Genesis*, JPS Torah Commentary (Philadelphia: Jewish Publication Society, 1989), 4; Gordon J. Wenham, *Rethinking Genesis 1–11: Gateway to the Bible* (Eugene, OR: Cascade Books, 2015), 5.

2. Sarna, *Genesis*, 4; Wenham, *Rethinking Genesis 1–11*, 4.

There is also a balance between plants on one side and animals and human beings on the other side in the narrative. God gives instructions to be fruitful and multiply only to the animals and human beings, and only to them does he give the plants for food (1:22, 28). Human beings are to eat the plants that yield seed and the fruit of trees, whereas animals on the land and in the sky are to eat "every green plant" (1:29–30). Everything inhabits a peaceful order, and the emphasis on the provision of plants for the food of every living creature hints that there is no violence among the creatures that have "the breath of life" (1:30).[3]

Within this peaceful order, human beings, both male and female, inhabit the most important place. Before creating them, God summons the other transcendent beings in his presence—or perhaps the other persons in the Trinity—to join him in what he is about to do: "Let us make man," he says, "in our image, after our likeness" (1:26).[4] Human beings alone, in their two genders, are made in God's image (1:26–27). Moreover, they alone receive from God the authority to rule over all the earth and its animals, a mandate so important that the narrative mentions it twice (1:26, 28). The second mention is its fullest form:

> Be fruitful and multiply and fill the earth and subdue it, and have dominion over the fish of the sea and over the birds of the heavens and over every living thing that moves on the earth.

Only after the final creative act of bringing a man and woman into existence and giving them this critical mandate is God's work of creation finished. God can then pronounce all his creation not merely "good" but "very good" (1:31).

---

3. Wenham, *Rethinking Genesis 1–11*, 16, 27.
4. Wenham, *Rethinking Genesis 1–11*, 14–15.

It is not the sixth day, the day of humanity's creation, however, that is the most important day. That honor goes to the seventh day. God blesses the seventh day and sets it apart from all the other days because it is a day of rest for him after the work of creation is finished (2:1–3).[5] This move implies a second mandate for human beings, and it is closely related to the first mandate. If human beings are created in God's image, then their raising of human families and their exercise of dominion over the earth correspond naturally to God's work in six days. God's rest on the seventh day implies that they, too, should not work constantly because they are designed for regular periods of rest.[6]

According to Genesis 1:1–2:3, then, God created a world of perfect harmony and peace with human beings as the crowning achievement of his creative work. This world corresponded to God's own peaceful and gracious character. It was ordered under the watchful care of the man and woman whom God had made in his own image and for whom he had generously provided. God in his goodness gave the man and woman the meaningful role of ruling over the animals, and he supplied the green plants as food for them all. Also in his goodness, God provided his human creation a pattern to follow in doing the work that he had given them. They were to work for six days, and then, on the seventh day, like him, they were to rest.

What Happened to God's Good Creation?

The next major section of Genesis (2:4–4:26) describes how this perfect world became the world as all humanity experiences it—a place of hostility between humans and animals (3:15), of pain in childbearing (3:16), of difficulty in obtaining food (3:17–19a), and of

---

5. Cf. Wenham, *Rethinking Genesis 1–11*, 16.
6. Wenham, *Rethinking Genesis 1–11*, 16.

death (3:19b), anger, violence, and oppression (4:1–26).[7] The section begins by returning to the period before God finished his creative work and focusing in greater detail on God's creation of and provision for human beings (2:4–25). By putting this section of God's work under the microscope, the narrative supplies the necessary background for its description of human disobedience to God and the suffering that this fateful decision entailed.

The first part of this new section, then, describes God's creation of the first man and of a beautiful garden within the otherwise uncultivated and largely arid land that he had previously created. God fashions the first man from the "dust" or the "clay" of the earth like a potter might make a pot on the wheel. Then, unlike any other potter, God breathes on his clay man, and he comes to life (2:7).

The rest of this first part of the story is told to emphasize the lavish way that God provided for humanity's well-being.[8] God provides a home for the man in a special enclosed area within the land of Eden. This park or garden contains "every tree that is pleasant to the sight and good for food" (2:9). A river flowing into the garden supplies plentiful water, and the area in which the garden is located is rich with beautiful metals, aromatic resins, and stones—gold, bdellium, onyx (2:12; cf. Ezek. 28:13). The most important provision for the man, however, is the woman God made from the man's rib. She is a suitable helper for him (Gen. 2:20) and affords the complement necessary for humanity to "be fruitful and multiply and fill the earth" (1:28). Working together, the man and woman will "work . . . and keep" the garden (2:15) and continue to exercise dominion over the animals (1:26, 28), a project Adam started when he named them (2:19–20). The man and the woman are naked but not ashamed.

---

7. Sarna, *Genesis*, 16.
8. Wenham, *Rethinking Genesis 1–11*, 26; Wenham, *Genesis 1–15*, Word Biblical Commentary 1 (Nashville: Thomas Nelson, 1987), 87.

Later, nakedness in the presence of others will be embarrassing, and it will be improper in the presence of God (3:7; Ex. 20:26; 28:42–43), but now, because the man and the woman are in exactly the relationship with God and others that God created them to have, there is no hint of any impropriety in their nakedness.[9]

This part of the story implies two further mandates for the man and the woman beyond the mandates to rule over the animal world and to rest on the Sabbath. A third mandate is to trust in God's goodness. This mandate emerges from the command that God gives to the man after he has created him and placed him in the garden. God had created two special trees in the garden, the tree of life and the tree of the knowledge of good and evil (Gen. 2:9). The tree of life conferred immortality on those who ate from it (3:22). In the same way, the tree of the knowledge of good and evil must have had some real power to confer knowledge on Adam.

What is this knowledge? The text does not explicitly say, but in subsequent years, after Adam and Eve have eaten from the forbidden tree, knowledge does grow among their descendants, some of it good and some of it evil.[10] Adam and Eve figure out how to cover themselves by sewing fig leaves together (3:7). They gain knowledge of evil when their son Cain kills his brother Abel and when Cain himself becomes a fugitive, far away, east of Eden (4:1–16; cf. 4:25). A descendant named Jabal becomes "the father of those who dwell in tents and have livestock" (4:20). His brother Jubal becomes "the father of all those who play the lyre and pipe" (4:21). Their half-brother, Tubal-cain, develops "all instruments of bronze and iron" (4:22).

Knowledge, then, does increase, but why does God consider it wrong to desire such knowledge? The text does not say explic-

---

9. Cf. Wenham, *Genesis 1–15*, 72, 87–88.
10. Sarna, *Genesis*, 19.

itly, but it seems likely that God wants his human creatures to be satisfied with the provision he himself has made for them and to continue to trust him to provide for them in the future. As Gordon Wenham has argued, God especially wants the man and woman to trust him with the knowledge of what is morally best for them—to realize, in the words of Proverbs 1:7, that "the fear of the Lord is the beginning of knowledge" and that only "fools despise wisdom and instruction."[11] To seek knowledge of good and evil on their own, therefore, is to seek autonomy. It is to say to God that human beings can survive very well apart from God's provision and instruction. Eating the forbidden fruit and seeking the knowledge it supplies is a movement away from God and toward independence from him. It is, in the words of the serpent later in the narrative, an effort to be "like God" in the sense that they will make decisions about good and evil for themselves (Gen. 3:5). God's command not to eat from the tree of the knowledge of good and evil is, therefore, both sensible and gracious.

The form of the command itself reveals something about God's character and the nature of his instruction to human beings. It begins with a positive emphasis on all that God has provided for his human creatures, "You may surely eat of every tree of the garden" (2:16), and then moves to the prohibition, "but of the tree of the knowledge of good and evil you shall not eat, for in the day that you eat of it you shall surely die" (2:17). So the form of the command is designed to encourage the man's trust in God. God has lavishly provided for his needs and generously permitted him to eat of nearly every tree of the garden. We learn later that even the tree of the knowledge of good and evil is "a delight to the eyes" (3:6). So every tree is beautiful and pleasing, and every tree but one is permitted to the man for food.

---

11. Wenham, *Genesis 1–15*, 63–64.

When God moves to the prohibition against eating from the tree, therefore, the man has every reason to believe that God has made the fruit of this tree off limits for the man's own good. The prohibition against eating from the tree of the knowledge of good and evil is essentially a mandate to trust God, and especially to trust that the instructions he gives his human creatures are for their own good.

The fourth and final implied mandate in the creation narrative comes just before the story takes a sinister turn with the introduction of the crafty serpent. It is a mandate that describes what should be the human response to God's creation of humanity in two perfectly complementary sexes, male and female, man and woman. This complementarity is worked out most fully in marriage, a bond so strong that it breaks the bond of previous family loyalties and creates a new family unit. Wenham points out that the words "a man shall leave his father and his mother and hold fast to his wife" (2:24) are "an astounding declaration in a world where filial duty was the most sacred obligation next to loyalty to God."[12]

In marriage, then, a single man and a single woman, each from his or her own family, become one flesh, and a new family begins. The mandate here is not that every man and woman should marry, nor is there any suggestion that a man or woman is not fully human unless married. Rather, the mandate is that human beings generally should be fruitful and multiply by means of family units established in marriage and that the same harmony existing in creation should exist in these family units as husband and wife complement each other.

In Genesis 1:1–2:24, then, God both creates and lavishly provides for human beings, the crown jewel of his creation and the only part of his creation made in his own image. He provides both their physical

---

12. Wenham, *Genesis 1–15*, 88.

needs and their need for purpose and guidance. He gives them food to eat and gives them the responsibility of exercising dominion over the animals. Their food comes to them in the form of plants, and therefore without violence, and their work is regularly interspersed with rest, and therefore without greed and exploitation. Their living environment is beautiful, and God gives them free range within it, with merely one limitation. The first man and woman, moreover, like all men and women after them, are to work together in harmony and establish new family units through monogamous marriage.

In 3:1–4:26, the narrator tells the story of how all this changes, and the focus of this next part of the narrative is on the first couple's disobedience to God's command not to eat from the tree of the knowledge of good and evil. The man and the woman shift their trust from God to one of God's creatures and then to their own ingenuity. In the process, they assert their independence from the Creator of all things who has so graciously provided for them.

The narrative is clear that the serpent who approaches the woman is one of the "beasts of the field" that "the LORD God had made" (3:1, 14). Later, the Scriptures identify the serpent with "the devil," or "Satan" (Rev. 12:9; 20:2), but here the focus is on his status as one of the land animals that God has formed out of the ground and over which God has given the man dominion (Gen. 1:26, 28; 2:19). Here the serpent disturbs the order of creation and, very incrementally, exercises dominion first over the woman and then, in a chain reaction, over the man.

God presumably made the serpent "crafty"—not necessarily a bad quality (see Prov. 12:16; 13:16, where the Hebrew word for "crafty" is translated "prudent")—but the serpent uses his craftiness to upset the divine order.[13] It is clear from his first comment to the

---

13. On the term translated "crafty" here, see Wenham, *Genesis 1–15*, 72.

woman that he intends to lead her to disobey God's command not to eat from the tree of the knowledge of good and evil. In accord with his craftiness, however, he never actually instructs her to disobey.[14] His approach is much more subtle. He simply misquotes what God actually said to the man in the prohibition and implies that since God has "said" this, he is not gracious and generous but miserly and insecure in his own position.

God had said this to the man:

> You may surely eat of every tree of the garden, but of the tree of the knowledge of good and evil you shall not eat, for in the day that you eat of it you shall surely die. (Gen. 2:16–17)

The serpent, however, misquotes God with a hint of feigned amazement:

> Did God actually say, "You shall not eat of any tree in the garden"? (3:1)

The serpent is not asking whether he has understood God's command correctly. He is subtly misrepresenting both the nature of God's command and the nature of God himself. What God "commanded" the man becomes in the serpent's mouth something that God merely "said."[15] His misquotation of the command itself, moreover, wildly distorts God's gracious character, and he then expresses surprise that God would be so tightfisted. Like a politician who brazenly accuses his opponent of weakness on precisely her strongest point, the serpent has shrewdly left out the positive and gracious preface to the actual prohibition. On the serpent's lips, God's gracious command becomes an expression of Scrooge-like stinginess.

---

14. Wenham, *Genesis 1–15*, 88.
15. Sarna, *Genesis*, 24.

The woman's reply to the serpent shows that his subtle strategy has already started to work. She does correct the serpent's "misunderstanding," but the serpent's suggestion that God is miserly has influenced her. As Wenham points out, her correction tones down the generosity of God's original statement, "You may surely eat of every tree of the garden . . ." (2:16), so that it now becomes the less lavish "We may eat of the fruit of the trees in the garden" (3:2).[16] God *did* make *some* fruit trees available to them, she seems to be saying, whereas actually God had made *every* tree in the orchard available to them but one.

Even that tree, moreover, was available to them for everything but food. God had said nothing about not touching the tree, only about not eating from it. The man and woman were presumably welcome to enjoy the "delight" of its beauty (3:6). The woman, however, characterizes God as stingier than he really is: "But God said, 'You shall not eat of the fruit of the tree that is in the midst of the garden, *neither shall you touch it*, lest you die'" (3:3). She is beginning to take her view of God from the serpent.

Perhaps emboldened by his success, the serpent directly contradicts the sanction that had accompanied God's command.[17] God had said of the tree, "In the day that you eat of it you shall surely die" (2:17), but the serpent tells the woman, "You will not surely die" (3:4). He then supplies a reason for the obvious question, "But why would God lie about this?" The reason he lied, according to the serpent, is that God knew that the fruit of the tree would give knowledge of good and evil to the man and woman, and this would make them like God. The serpent seems to assume that the man and woman are not like God and that God does not want them to be like him. This, in turn, implies that God's unique position of power and authority in

---

16. Wenham, *Genesis 1–15*, 73.
17. Sarna, *Genesis*, 25.

the universe were conferred on him by his superior knowledge and that he is insecure in this position. The serpent seems to think that God, the man, and the woman are separate and competing individuals and that God feels threatened by the possible encroachment of the man and woman on his space.

This is a far cry from reality. God created the man and the woman in his own image (1:26–27; 5:1). In this sense, he created them to be "like him." He enjoys their company as he interacts with them (2:19) and walks among them (3:8) in the garden he has graciously provided to meet all their needs. It is true that they are not like God with respect to his knowledge, but God withheld the knowledge of good and evil from them for their own good. He arranged things so that they would rely on his goodness for their well-being and have a relationship of trust with him.

When both the woman and the man eat the fruit, therefore, they assert their independence from God. They demonstrate their desire to make their way in the world on the basis of their own knowledge, apart from God's provision for them, including his revelation to them of what is best for them. Most significant of all, they end their relationship of trust with him.

The immediate impact of their disobedience is alienation from God and alienation from each other. Their alienation from God is evident in their fearful efforts to hide themselves from him (Gen. 3:8–10). Their alienation from each other is clear from the blame game that ensues when God asks the man, "Have you eaten of the tree of which I commanded you not to eat?" (3:11). The man immediately tries to shift responsibility to the woman and to God: "The woman whom you gave to be with me, she gave me fruit of the tree, and I ate" (3:12). Although the man was present during the entire interchange between his wife and the serpent (3:6), he spares the serpent and himself, blaming everything first on God, who gave him his wife, and then on the woman. The delight that prompted him to cry out, "This at last is bone of my bones / and flesh of my flesh" (2:23), now turns to self-centeredness as he tries to throw his perfectly suited companion under the bus. The woman, more sensibly but with no more inclination than the man to be honest about accepting the blame, fingers the serpent as the culprit (3:13).

The death that God had said would ensue on the day that the man ate from the forbidden tree now begins, and God describes what form this death will take for them all—beast, woman, man, and all their descendants (3:14–19).[18] It is not a literal death before the sun sets but the beginning both of human mortality and of the spiritual death that accompanies banishment from the presence of God.

Now, rather than harmony between the human and animal world, there will often be enmity, typified in the enmity between the serpent, the woman, and the human offspring that will come from her (3:14–15). Rather than the delight and partnership that once characterized man and wife (2:20–25), there will be selfish desire and the tendency to dominate (3:16). Rather than receiving vegetables and fruit for food easily and focusing on their task of exercising dominion over the animals (1:26, 28–29; 2:9, 16), God's human creatures will work hard for their sustenance. The earth will work against them, producing thorns and thistles that will choke their crops, and they will be able to control the earth's opposition only by hard manual labor. In the end, however, the earth will win. God will not permit the man and woman to eat from the tree of life (3:22), and so they will die physically, returning to the dust from which God had fashioned the man (3:17–19; cf. 2:7).

After pronouncing these judgments, God expels the man from the garden. The garden had been a holy sanctuary—a sort of temple—

---

18. Wenham, *Genesis 1–15*, 83, 90.

in which God met personally with his human creatures.[19] But they chose the path of alienation from their Creator, and in accord with this choice, he expels them from his presence.

As the story of creation's beauty and brokenness draws to a close, the narrative reveals not only the fulfillment of God's curses on the serpent, the woman, and the man but also the trajectory of human relationships with God and one another, which, if God does not intervene, only move from bad to worse.[20] Cain is not merely afraid of God, as was Adam (3:10), but is angry with God (4:5). His unjustified anger leads not merely to blame shifting, as it did with Adam (3:12), but to murder (4:8)—and a murder that completely ignores God's warning about sin "crouching at the door," desiring Cain and ready to consume him (4:6–8). Neither Adam nor Eve complain about God's punishment of expulsion from the garden for their disobedience, but Cain whines bitterly that his similar punishment "is greater than I can bear" (4:13).

Near the story's end is a brief account of Cain's descendant Lamech, who illustrates how far humanity has traveled from the ideal of existence in the presence of God in the peaceful garden he had provided. "Lamech took two wives" (4:19), a violation of God's implied mandate that human society should be organized through the peaceful partnership and complementarity of one man and one woman (2:24). The snapshot we get of Lamech's life and character does not bode well for these women—or anyone else in his field of power. He blurts out a trash-talking poem, addressed to his two wives, whom we can imagine cowering in terror as Lamech announces that he killed "a young man" (perhaps a child?) for merely hitting him and

---

19. Wenham, *Genesis 1–15*, 90; Wenham, *Rethinking Genesis 1–11*, 28–29. See also G. K. Beale, *The Temple and the Church's Mission: A Biblical Theology of the Dwelling Place of God*, New Studies in Biblical Theology 17 (Downers Grove, IL: InterVarsity Press, 2004), 66–80; T. Desmond Alexander, *The City of God and the Goal of Creation*, Short Studies in Biblical Theology (Wheaton, IL: Crossway, 2018), 16–20.

20. Wenham, *Genesis 1–15*, 100; Wenham, *Rethinking Genesis 1–11*, 21–22.

that if anyone tries to harm him, he will retaliate ten times more severely than anything associated with his ancestor Cain (4:23–24).

Why would Lamech say this to his wives ("Adah and Zillah, hear my voice; / you wives of Lamech, listen to what I say," 4:23)? Is it perhaps a warning to them of the domestic violence they will experience unless they do exactly as he says?[21] This is a far cry from the beautiful piece of delighted poetry that the first man sings about, and presumably to, his wife on their wedding day in 2:23:

> This at last is bone of my bones
>> and flesh of my flesh;
> she shall be called Woman,
>> because she was taken out of Man.

Adam and Eve, therefore, through their failure to trust the goodness and generosity of God, pointed humanity in a direction that would lead to ever-greater distance from God and his instructions about how he created human beings to live. This alienation from God and his word would, in turn, lead to the increasing alienation of human beings from one another and from the earth that God created to sustain them.

Hints of Hope

There are, however, hints of hope within this sad story. One of the main hints lies simply in the character of the God who created the world. His immense generosity in providing for his human creatures and his clear desire to live in a close, trusting relationship with them suggest that God is unlikely to give up on humanity after their act of defiant self-assertion. This notion receives confirmation from the ways in which God continues to communicate with and help his

---

21. I owe this suggestion to my pastor, Brad Allison.

creatures despite their banishment from his presence. Before he sends them out from the garden, he makes proper and substantial clothing for them from animal skins (Gen. 3:21) to replace their flimsy fig-tree leaves, incompetently sewn together to hide their nakedness.[22]

God's expulsion from the garden of the man and woman (now called Adam and Eve) is probably also a merciful act. To allow them to prolong their lives forever in their state of alienation from God and discord with each other by eating from the garden's tree of life will bring only endless suffering. Like Gollum in J. R. R. Tolkien's *Lord of the Rings*, man and woman will be in danger of devolving into an ever-deepening and destructive self-centeredness as the generations pass.

The Lord's willingness to accept Abel's offering (4:4), his attempt to provide Cain with instruction about the insidious nature of sin (4:6–7), the mercy that he shows to Cain even after Cain has refused to pay attention to him (4:15), and the kindness of the Lord in granting Adam and Eve another child after Abel's murder (4:25–26) all indicate that God has not abandoned even those who have rejected him. In addition to kindnesses such as these, God's human creation continues to bear God's image, to possess God's mandate to rule over the earth's animals, and to benefit (when they obey them) from God's mandates to balance work with rest and to organize human society around the marriage partnership of one man and one woman.

Although in Psalm 8 God has enemies that must be stilled (8:2), the psalmist can still praise the majestic name of the Lord on the basis of his creation (8:1). He can still express amazement that God has crowned human beings with glory and honor (8:4–5) and given them dominion over the animals (8:6–8). Similarly, in Psalm 104, the psalmist praises the Lord for the wonders of the natural world,

---

22. Wenham says that the attempt to sew fig-tree leaves together as clothing suggests "urgency and desperation." *Genesis 1–15*, 76.

including the blessings that God has provided to human beings in creation—plants to cultivate for their food, wine to make their hearts glad, oil to beautify their faces, bread to give them strength, and the moon and sun to regulate their work (104:14–15, 23). Psalm 104 ends with a prayer that "sinners" will be "consumed from the earth" and "the wicked" will "be no more" (104:35), but the world is still a majestic and wonderful place that points to its Creator and to the grace and goodness he has shown humanity.

Conclusion

By the end of Genesis 4, then, the world is a complex mixture of God's gracious, undeserved blessing and the grim results of human rebellion against God. The man and the woman have turned away from the trust that they once had in God and his goodness and have placed their confidence instead in their own ingenuity. God has allowed them and their descendants to go their own way with all the consequences that doing so entails. They can no longer live in God's presence, and discord among themselves has gone from bad to worse. The direction of humanity by the end of Genesis 4 is clearly one of ever-greater alienation from God and more and more social violence and disintegration. Their newly gained knowledge of good and evil has not improved the lot of human beings but pushed humanity far down the road of self-destruction.

Human society, left to its own devices, has not improved in the many years since that fateful conversation with the serpent. Despite the beauty and blessing of our world, it is still a place marked by an unwillingness to trust in, or often even to believe in the existence of, God. Human society, moreover, is characterized by greed, hatred, and violence on a scale so massive that the health of the entire planet is threatened and that there seems to be no end in sight to human suffering. The Scriptures, however, do not leave us there.

2

Hints at a Solution

As God's gracious character in Genesis 1–4 might lead us to suspect, he does not abandon his human creatures, although "the wickedness of man [is] great in the earth" and "every intention of the thoughts of his heart [is] only evil continually" (Gen. 6:5; cf. 8:21). Rather than allow humanity to persist in their alienation from him and from one another, God immediately begins to work among his human creatures to form a group of people who will trust him and will, through their lives of trust, call the rest of the world back to their Creator.

God Creates a People for Himself

God begins this process by revealing himself to a Chaldean named Abraham, giving him instructions to travel to a particular land that will become his family's possession and expressing his intention to bless Abraham and his descendants. In addition, God says that he intends to bless "all the families of the earth" through Abraham (Gen. 12:3).

God is faithful to his promise and cares for Abraham's extended family through both personal struggles, such as barrenness, and difficulties that affect the entire clan, such as famine (21:1–7; 45:1–28). Eventually, through the cruelty of the rulers of Egypt, Abraham's family is reduced to slavery, outside the land that God had promised to give him (Ex. 1:8–22). God rescues Abraham's descendants from this oppression through a leader named Moses, an event known as "the exodus" (cf. 12:1–50). Through this rescue God formally constitutes his now vast people as the nation of Israel.

According to the book of Exodus, God instructs Moses to bear this message from him to Israel:

> You yourselves have seen what I did to the Egyptians, and how I bore you on eagles' wings and brought you to myself. Now therefore, if you will indeed obey my voice and keep my covenant, you shall be my treasured possession among all peoples, for all the earth is mine; and you shall be to me a kingdom of priests and a holy nation. (19:4–6)

Three elements of this momentous statement are particularly important. First, God begins by reminding Israel of the gracious nature of his character. Before saying anything about their obligation to obey him and to keep the solemn agreement they are about to enter with him, he recalls his dramatic rescue of them from slavery in Egypt.

Second, the statement describes a certain tension between the special nature of God's own treasured people and God's sovereignty over the whole earth. All the earth is God's, but Israel occupies a particularly special place among the nations of the earth.

Third, the statement describes the reason why God has chosen Israel from the nations of the earth and is about to enter into a solemn agreement—or "covenant"—with them. They are to be "a kingdom of priests and a holy nation." The entire nation, then, not simply a

certain group within it, is to adopt a priestly role and to be "holy"—
that is, "singled out"—from others.[1]

To whom are they to act as priests? Why are they singled out from
others to fulfill this mission? The text does not say explicitly, but since
God has just mentioned that "all the earth" belongs to him, it seems
likely that God gives to Israel the special task of serving as priests to
the surrounding world.[2] As the details of the law that Israel is expected
to obey unfold in the coming chapters and in the books of Leviticus,
Numbers, and Deuteronomy, it becomes clear that Israel is to live before the world in a way that models God's own character. He created
human beings to acknowledge him alone as God; to love him with
all their heart, soul, mind, and strength (Deut. 6:4–5); and to love
their neighbors as themselves (Lev. 19:18). Israel's mission is to show
the world, by the way it lives as a society, what it means to live in the
way God designed human beings to live. As God puts it to Israel in
Leviticus 11:45, "I am the LORD who brought you up out of the land
of Egypt to be your God. You shall therefore be holy, for I am holy."

Failure and Hope

Twice in these books of the law God goes into detail about the blessings Israel will experience if it obeys God's instructions (Lev. 26:3–
12; Deut. 28:1–14) and the curses it will experience if it disobeys
(Lev. 26:14–45; Deut. 28:15–68). In Leviticus 26:3–12, the blessings
for obedience sound a lot like life in the garden of Eden before Adam
and Eve disobeyed God. There will be abundant rain for crops; the
trees will bear fruit (26:4). Agriculture will be so easy and the yields

---

1. Ludwig Koehler and Walter Baumgartner, *The Hebrew and Aramaic Lexicon of the Old Testament*, rev. Walter Baumgartner and Johann Jakob Stamm, study ed., 2 vols. (Leiden: Brill, 2001), 2:1066.
2. Nahum M. Sarna, *Exodus*, JPS Torah Commentary (Philadelphia: Jewish Publication Society, 1991), 104; Douglas K. Stuart, *Exodus*, New American Commentary 2 (Nashville: Broad-man and Holman, 2006), 423; Christopher J. H. Wright, *The Mission of God: Unlocking the Bible's Grand Narrative* (Downers Grove, IL: IVP Academic, 2006), 224–25.

so abundant that people will thresh their grain until it is time for the grape harvest, and the grape harvest will last until it is time to plant grain again (26:5). In addition to abundant food, there will be peace in the form of both safety from dangerous animals and safety from opposing armies (26:6–8). God will cause his people to "be fruitful and multiply," just as he intended for his human creation to multiply according to Genesis 1:26 and 28 (Lev. 26:9). Just as he did in the garden of Eden (Gen. 2:19; 3:8), God will make his dwelling with his people and will walk among them (Lev. 26:11–12).

In both Leviticus 26 and Deuteronomy 28, however, the blessings for obedience to the law are brief and general compared to the lengthy and more specific curses for disobedience. A comparison of the curses for disobedience with the subsequent history of Israel reveals that even as God gives this law to Israel, he knows they will disobey it. Both passages describe Israel's devastation at the hands of foreign powers and their exile from their own land to foreign territories (Lev. 26:27–39; Deut. 28:25–68), events that actually happen in later years. As a nation, then, Israel fails at the mission God has given them—to be a kingdom of priests and a holy nation. Rather than standing apart from the nations that surround them and bearing witness by their way of life to the character of God, many Israelites, often under the leadership of wicked kings, join the surrounding nations in worshiping false gods and in practicing injustice, particularly toward the poor. Like Adam and Eve before them, they reject God's instruction and choose to go their own way.

The problem certainly lies not with Israel alone but with a human tendency to rebel against God that has infected everyone since the original couple's disobedience to God's command. Just as "every intention of the thoughts of" the human heart is "only evil continually" (Gen. 6:5; cf. 8:21), so Israel's heart is also corrupt. As Israel is on the verge of entering the land that God has promised to Abraham, and forty years after God has given the law to Israel, Moses says to them, "To this day the Lord has not given you a heart to understand or eyes to see or ears to hear" (Deut. 29:4).

Nevertheless, the law itself sounds a note of hope that God one day will change Israel's heart, so that his people will follow him faithfully, both in the devotion they show to him and in the way they treat one another. At the end of its list of curses for disobedience to the law, Leviticus says this:

> But if they confess their iniquity and the iniquity of their fathers in their treachery that they committed against me, and also in walking contrary to me, so that I walked contrary to them and brought them into the land of their enemies—if then their uncircumcised heart is humbled and they make amends for their iniquity, then I will remember my covenant with Jacob, and I will remember my covenant with Isaac and my covenant with Abraham, and I will remember the land. (Lev. 26:40–42)

Deuteronomy clarifies that this necessary change of heart can come only at God's initiative but that it will certainly come. It envisions a future when Israel has experienced both the blessing and the curse outlined in 28:1–68 (30:1) but mainly the curse, which has taken the form of exile (28:25–68; 29:22–28). After that exile, according to 30:1–10, Israel will return to the Lord and obey what Moses has commanded them "with all [their] heart and with all [their] soul" (30:1–2). The Lord will then gather Israel from the various lands where the conquering nations have exiled them (30:3–5). This change of heart will come from the Lord himself:

> The Lord your God will circumcise your heart and the heart of your offspring, so that you will love the Lord your God with all your heart and with all your soul, that you may live. (30:6)

Only God can solve the problem of the corrupt human heart (Gen. 6:5; 8:21) that has plagued all humanity, including Israel, from that fateful day in Eden forward. Deuteronomy 30:1–10 envisions a day when God will rescue Israel and the blessing of God will rest on his people permanently.[3]

Isaiah's Diagnosis of the Problem and Vision of God's Remedy

The prophet Isaiah adopts the same perspective but adds to it the further notion that God will restore Israel's relationship with him and return the whole earth and its peoples to an environment of justice, peace, abundance, and fellowship with the Creator. By Isaiah's time, Israel has become divided into two parts, a northern kingdom, commonly called Israel, and a southern kingdom, called Judah. Isaiah ministers during a turbulent period in Judah's history (745–612 BC) when the powerful and ruthless Assyrian Empire first threatens the northern kingdom, which it soon transforms into one of its own provinces, and then for a much longer period threatens Isaiah's home city of Jerusalem and the people of Judah, often doing them significant harm.[4]

In this environment of international upheaval, Isaiah consistently urges Israel to trust its future to the Lord rather than to humanly constructed alliances with the surrounding nations and with the false gods to whom these nations entrust their own destiny. God makes it clear to Isaiah, however, that most of Israel will not heed his words of warning. The majority will hear but not understand and see but

---

3. See J. G. McConville, *Grace in the End: A Study of Deuteronomic Theology*, Studies in Old Testament Biblical Theology (Grand Rapids, MI: Zondervan, 1993), 134–39; McConville, *Deuteronomy*, Apollos Old Testament Commentary (Downers Grove, IL: InterVarsity Press, 2002), 425–28.

4. Paul R. House, *Isaiah*, Mentor Commentary, 2 vols. (Fearn, Ross-shire, Scotland: Mentor, 2019), 1:24, 47.

not perceive his message (Isa. 6:9; cf. Deut. 29:4), and their spiritual obtuseness and unfaithfulness will lead to almost total destruction (Isa. 6:11–12). A "holy seed" will remain, however, and that seed will form a "stump" (6:13)—a stump that promises the possibility of new growth.

Isaiah views the anxiety and violence that Assyria is producing among God's people as part of the curse that justly comes to them because of their disobedience to the Mosaic law (5:24; 42:24). At one point, the Lord says,

> Oh that you had paid attention to my commandments!
> Then your peace would have been like a river,
> and your righteousness like the waves of the sea. (48:18)

Isaiah also makes it clear that this pattern of disobedience and curse is something that afflicts not only Israel but the whole earth:

> The earth lies defiled
> under its inhabitants;
> for they have transgressed the laws,
> violated the statutes,
> broken the everlasting covenant.
> Therefore a curse devours the earth,
> and its inhabitants suffer for their guilt;
> therefore the inhabitants of the earth are scorched
> and few men are left. (24:5–6)

The prophet interlaces his visions of disobedience and suffering, however, with beautiful visions of a wonderful future.[5] This will be a future in which the "holy seed" or "stump" left after God's judgment will grow and flourish. God will not merely restore Israel's political

---

5. House, *Isaiah*, 1:27–32.

and spiritual fortunes but, through Israel, will restore peace, justice, and fellowship with himself to all the nations of the earth. The earth will return to the place of abundance and security that it was when God created it, and justice will prevail throughout human society. Isaiah's book begins with a plea to the heavens and the earth to bear witness to his testimony to Israel's rebellion against the Lord (1:2), and it ends with a vision of a new heavens and a new earth populated by people from both Israel and all nations who worship the Lord as the one true God (66:22).

Isaiah's Rhythm of Judgment and Blessing

Isaiah's first four chapters provide a helpful introduction to the pattern of judgment and renewal that characterizes the whole book.[6] Israel, Isaiah says, neither knows nor understands the Lord who reared and brought it up, like a Father taking care of his child (Isa. 1:2). This puzzling obtuseness has affected Israel from head to toe and inside out. They are "laden with iniquity" and are "utterly estranged" from the Lord: "The whole head is sick, / and the whole heart is faint" (1:4–5). As a result, their destruction at the hands of the Assyrians has been almost total (1:7–8). The problem is that although Israel has been enthusiastic about the outward mechanics of their devotion to the Lord—offering sacrifice and observing sacred days—they have abandoned justice, practiced oppression, and neglected the needy (1:10–17, 23).

Some of them, at least, have also been playing false with the Lord and trying their hand at worshiping other gods in the oak groves and gardens where the shrines of those gods are located (1:29–30). They

---

6. In my discussion of Isaiah, I have followed House's analysis of its structure as a series of seven prophecies, each speaking mainly of God's judgment but each also ending in a hopeful description of God's people finally at rest in his presence in Zion. "Zion" is the hill in Jerusalem on which the temple was located and is, for Isaiah, symbolic of God's presence with his people. House, *Isaiah*, 1:26–32.

have turned from worshiping the Creator to worshiping the natural world he has created.[7]

There is, nevertheless, hope, not simply for Israel but for all the world, through Israel's future faithfulness. Although Israel's sins in Isaiah's time are "like scarlet," one day they will be "as white as snow" (1:18), and one day the Lord will "smelt away" all the injustice, rebellion, and idolatry in Israel, restoring righteousness there so fully that Jerusalem will be "called the city of righteousness, the faithful city" (1:25–26). Jerusalem will be such a model of justice that the nations of the world will take notice and want to imitate its citizens' way of life. It will be as if the hill on which the temple in Jerusalem is located suddenly becomes the highest mountain on earth and "all the nations" (2:2) stream toward it, saying,

> Come, let us go up to the mountain of the LORD,
>> to the house of the God of Jacob,
> that he may teach us his ways
>> and that we may walk in his paths. (2:3)

In the end, justice and peace will prevail so thoroughly that the nations will "beat their swords into plowshares, / and their spears into pruning hooks" (2:4). Rather than war, there will be the peaceful pursuit of agriculture, a thought that recalls the safety and abundance of the garden in Eden.

Just as Deuteronomy ends its vision of a renewed Israel with a call to "choose life, that you and your offspring may live" (Deut. 30:19), so Isaiah ends this cycle of judgment and hope with a call to Israel to take the step necessary for the wonderful vision he has just described to become reality: "Come," he says to them, "let us walk / in the light of the LORD" (Isa. 2:5).

---

7. House, *Isaiah*, 1:63–64.

Isaiah then repeats the same judgment-and-blessing pattern, and once again, his rebuke gives way to a vision of abundance and safety that recalls the safety of the garden of Eden and the ideal description in Leviticus 26:3–12 of God's blessings for the obedient:

> In that day the branch of the LORD shall be beautiful and glorious, and the fruit of the land shall be the pride and honor of the survivors of Israel. And he who is left in Zion and remains in Jerusalem will be called holy, everyone who has been recorded for life in Jerusalem, when the Lord shall have washed away the filth of the daughters of Zion and cleansed the bloodstains of Jerusalem from its midst by a spirit of judgment and by a spirit of burning. Then the LORD will create over the whole site of Mount Zion and over her assemblies a cloud by day, and smoke and the shining of a flaming fire by night; for over all the glory there will be a canopy. There will be a booth for shade by day from the heat, and for a refuge and a shelter from the storm and rain. (Isa. 4:2–6)

Here Isaiah envisions Israel as a holy people, purified of their wickedness and living in a land of abundance and safety. Crops will be fruitful. The Lord will "create" again, just as he did when he created the heavens and the earth.

In this instance, what the Lord will create recalls the time when he led Israel out of slavery in Egypt and provided them with a cloud of shade by day and a guiding pillar of fire by night.[8] These echoes of Israel's rescue from slavery communicate that in the future time of restoration, God will be present with his people and will provide for them, just as he was present and provided during the exodus and in the garden of Eden before the first couple's disobedience.[9]

---

8. House, *Isaiah*, 1:118.
9. On Isaiah's imagery here as signs of God's presence, see House, *Isaiah*, 1:118.

The Davidic King as the Agent of Blessing

Isaiah's second major cycle of judgment and eventual restoration (Isa. 5:1–12:6) begins by drawing an analogy between untrusting and disobedient Israel and an unfruitful vineyard (5:1–7). Like a disappointed farmer who finds bad fruit in a vineyard he has worked hard to tend, God

> looked for justice,
>> but behold, bloodshed;
> for righteousness,
>> but behold, an outcry! (5:7)

A little later in the section, the Lord gives a sign to the unbelieving King Ahaz, a descendant of the greatest king of the united kingdom of Israel, King David. A "virgin," he says, "shall conceive and bear a son, and shall call his name Immanuel" (7:14). "Immanuel" is Hebrew for "God is with us." Later still, Isaiah describes the birth of a child who will bring an end to the contempt that "the land of Zebulun and the land of Naphtali" in the region of Galilee (9:1) felt after "Tiglath-pileser king of Assyria came and captured" them during Isaiah's time (2 Kings 15:29). This child, however, is no temporary or even temporal ruler. He will be called

> Wonderful Counselor, Mighty God,
>> Everlasting Father, Prince of Peace,

and

> of the increase of his government and of peace
>> there will be no end.

He will rule "with justice and with righteousness" forever (Isa. 9:6–7).[10]

---

10. On the historical background, see House, *Isaiah*, 1:264–65.

Isaiah ends this series of descriptions of judgment and blessing with another, lengthier description of the coming Davidic king (11:1–12:6).[11] Since David's father was Jesse, Isaiah calls this great Davidic descendant poetically "a shoot from the stump of Jesse" (11:1; cf. 6:13). The idea of new growth from the stump of a downed tree implies that the new king will arise from the devastation Israel has experienced through its disobedience to God at the hands of the Assyrians (and, eventually, the Babylonians and the Romans). At the time of this king's coming, Israelites whom the Assyrians had uprooted from their homeland and settled in their own region will stream in large numbers back to Judah. Just as in 4:5, Isaiah compares this period of redemption to the exodus from Egypt:

> There will be a highway from Assyria
> > for the remnant that remains of his people,
> as there was for Israel
> > when they came up from the land of Egypt. (11:16)

The great Davidic king will possess two main character traits, the second arising from the first. First, he will have such a profound spiritual connection to the Lord that he will fully understand the Lord's will in any given instance and know precisely how to act in the most prudent way from the Lord's perspective (11:2). Second, he will be a perfectly fair, just, and equitable judge and decision maker. He will not favor the attractive or be swayed by the rumor mill (11:3). As a result, the poor and marginalized of the earth will receive a just verdict in court rather than a verdict tilted against them (11:4). Righteousness and honesty will be such an important part of this king's character that Isaiah speaks of these virtues poetically as a belt around the king's waist (11:5). They will be like part of his clothing.

---

11. I am still following House's structural outline. *Isaiah*, 1:29.

This king will rule with such wisdom that creation will be restored to the peaceful existence it had before human disobedience. The nonviolent vegetarianism that Genesis 1–2 describes will again characterize the earth. The wolf, the leopard, the lion, and the bear will lose their appetite for meat and dwell in peace with the easiest catch of their natural prey—the lamb, the kid goat, the calf, and the fattened cow (Isa. 11:6–8). Wild and vicious animals will be domesticated to such an extent that a "little boy" (NASB) can herd them, and even the mighty lion will be satisfied with hay (11:6–7). The enmity between the serpent and humanity (Gen. 3:15) will end so that venomous snakes pose no threat to babies and toddlers (Isa. 11:8).

Peace in the animal world will be matched by peace at the societal level as the nations of the earth look to the great Davidic king for governance (11:9–16). Israel will be reunited, the nations that oppressed God's people will be conquered, and exiled Israelites will be restored to their homes. This life of restoration and peace will not be Israel's alone, moreover, but

> the earth shall be full of the knowledge of the LORD
> as the waters cover the sea. (11:9)

Israel itself will voice its praise to God before all the nations of the earth for the glorious things that he has done (12:4–5).

The Blessing of the Nations and the End of Death

Near the end of the third cycle of judgment and restoration (Isa. 13:1–27:13), Isaiah develops a similar vision of Israel, its people, and its land occupying the center of a renewed earth. Speaking of Mount Zion, in Jerusalem, the capital of Judah, Isaiah says this:

> On this mountain the LORD of hosts will make for all peoples
> a feast of rich food, a feast of well-aged wine,
> of rich food full of marrow, of aged wine well refined.

And he will swallow up on this mountain
    the covering that is cast over all peoples,
    the veil that is spread over all nations.
He will swallow up death forever;
and the Lord God will wipe away tears from all faces,
    and the reproach of his people he will take away from all
        the earth,
    for the Lord has spoken. (25:6–9; cf. 26:19)

Just as in the garden before the first couple's disobedience, God will provide plentiful food for his human creatures, and they will no longer be subject to the curse of death (Gen. 2:17; 3:17–19) with the sense of loss and sadness that death brings to those left behind. Just as God said to Abraham, moreover, all the nations of the earth will be blessed through Abraham's descendants as Israel emerges from the period of rebellion against God and his judgment of Israel through the oppression of the surrounding nations. A few paragraphs later Isaiah says,

In days to come, Jacob shall take root,
    Israel shall blossom and put forth shoots
    and fill the whole world with fruit. (Isa. 27:6)

A Righteous King and a Peaceful Existence

Within his fourth major section of judgment and blessing (Isa. 28:1–35:10), Isaiah moves back to a description of the great king who will enact this whole new order. Once again, the prophet emphasizes the righteousness of this king, although now he adds that there will be righteous "princes" underneath him who will also rule justly (32:1). The king and his subordinates will preside over a society in which those who have experienced injustice and oppression will find shelter as if from a strong wind or a storm (32:2). Fools and deceivers will no longer prevail against the poor and needy (32:3–8). God will pour out his Spirit on his people, and the justice and righteousness that will characterize society will be matched by fruitful fields, peace, righteousness, quietness, trust among people, and life "in secure dwellings, and in quiet resting places" (32:15–19). Recalling the scene of peaceful vegetarianism in Genesis 1–2, Isaiah says that people will "sow beside all waters" and will "let the feet of the ox and the donkey range free" (32:20).

At the end of the section, Isaiah describes God's rescue of Judah from the oppression of Edom, a vassal state of Assyria during this period and a traditional enemy of Judah on its southern border.[12] Edom had taken advantage of Judah's weakness in the late eighth century to carry away some of its people as captives, but God promised that such oppression would not last. Eventually,

> the eyes of the blind shall be opened,
>   and the ears of the deaf unstopped;
> then shall the lame man leap like a deer,
>   and the tongue of the mute sing for joy. (35:5–6)

Here, too, the imagery describes an idyllic setting in which physical affliction is healed.

God's Royal Servant

Later, within his fifth major section of judgment and blessing (Isa. 36:1–56:8), Isaiah refers to an individual whom the Lord calls "my servant" and who functions in much the same way as the coming Davidic king. God's Spirit is "upon him," and he will "bring forth justice to the nations" (42:1; cf. 49:1, 6; 52:15). He will not be a typical

---

12. On the historical background, see House, *Isaiah*, 2:158–60.

potentate of the period, violently conquering and oppressing the surrounding nations, but will be humble, gentle, and patient:[13]

> He will not cry aloud or lift up his voice,
>> or make it heard in the street;
> a bruised reed he will not break,
>> and a faintly burning wick he will not quench;
>> he will faithfully bring forth justice.
> He will not grow faint or be discouraged
>> till he has established justice in the earth;
>> and the coastlands wait for his law. (42:2–4; cf. 49:4;
>>> 52:14; 53:2–3, 7–9)

God prefaces his commission to his servant (42:6–9) with a reference
back to the creation of heaven, earth, and especially human beings:

> Thus says God, the LORD,
>> who created the heavens and stretched them out,
>> who spread out the earth and what comes from it,
> who gives breath to the people on it
>> and spirit to those who walk in it. (42:5)

The Lord then tells his servant that he will be "a covenant for the
people, / a light for the nations" (42:6), a poetic way of saying that the
servant will mediate between God and his people Israel and will also
reveal God's benevolent instruction to all the peoples of the earth.[14]
He will "open the eyes that are blind" and "bring out the prison-
ers from the dungeon" (42:7). Isaiah makes clear a few paragraphs
later that blindness and imprisonment are metaphorical ways of de-

---

13. Cf. John N. Oswalt, *The Book of Isaiah, Chapters 40–66*, New International Commentary on the Old Testament (Grand Rapids, MI: Eerdmans, 1998), 111.

14. See the NET translation: "I . . . make you a covenant mediator for people." Also see the comments of J. A. Alexander, *Commentary on the Prophecies of Isaiah*, ed. John Eadie, 2 vols. (New York: Scribner, Armstrong, 1878), 2:136.

scribing Israel's lack of knowledge and sinfulness (42:19, 22).[15] Here, however, Isaiah describes both Israel and the nations as blind and imprisoned. Everyone, whether Israelite or not, needs the gracious rescue God's servant will provide.

In another description of the servant a few chapters later (49:1–7), Isaiah makes a mysterious correlation between the servant and Israel. Here the servant plays the same role as the servant of 42:1–7.[16] He calls the coastlands and the peoples from afar to pay careful attention to him (49:1; cf. 42:1). He performs his mission with humility and without any obvious success from the perspective of the surrounding society (49:4; cf. 42:2–3). He calls Israel back to the Lord and follows that call with an extension of the light of the Lord to the nations (49:5–7; cf. 42:6). Yet in the middle of all this (49:3), the Lord says to the servant,

> You are my servant,
> 　Israel, in whom I will be glorified. (49:3)

At first it might seem that the mystery is easily solved: the servant is Israel! But how can Israel call Israel back to the Lord?[17] Clearly, the servant is an individual, like the great Davidic king of Isaiah 11, who calls both Israel and the nations into the light of God's revelation and eventual salvation (49:6) but who also completes the vocation that God had given to Israel when he constituted it as a nation. In the face of Israel's failure to be the means by which God will fulfill his promise to bless the nations through Abraham (Gen. 12:3), the servant will fulfill that promise. He will be the conduit of God's blessing, through Abraham, to all the nations of the earth. He will be "Israel" in this sense.

---

15. Oswalt, *Isaiah, Chapters 40–66*, 130–31.
16. Oswalt, *Isaiah, Chapters 40–66*, 288.
17. Oswalt, *Isaiah, Chapters 40–66*, 293.

Later still in this section, Isaiah becomes even more specific about how the servant will accomplish this. Isaiah has already led his readers to expect that the servant will not triumph in the same way as other kings of the period, with violence followed by proud assertions of power. He will not "cry aloud or lift up his voice" (Isa. 42:2). Even if his enemies had the vulnerability of a bruised reed or a faintly burning wick, he will neither break nor quench them (42:2–3). The servant will not put his confidence in his own labor or his strength but in the Lord whose commitment to justice he will trust (49:4).[18]

In 52:13–53:12, Isaiah fills out this picture of the servant's humility. In a way reminiscent of the great Davidic king in 11:1–2, the servant will be wise (52:13) and will spring like a young plant from dry ground (53:2), but like the servant in Isaiah 42 and 49, he will be so humble that it will be as if his appearance were marred and painful to see (52:14; 53:2–3). People will despise him, failing to recognize who he is (53:3) to the extent that, although he is innocent of any injustice, they will execute him as a criminal (53:7–9).

From this very miscarriage of justice, however, will come a transformation of Israel's relationship with God. The Lord's servant will experience the punishment Israel deserved, and this substitutionary punishment will bring them peace (53:5). The death of the righteous servant will make "many to be accounted righteous" (53:11). When the injustice and oppression of Israel reaches its lowest point, God will use that low point to begin the restoration of his people to a relationship with himself.

There are indications in this passage, moreover, that the forgiveness God offers to his people through the substitutionary death of his innocent servant will extend to the nations. In 52:15, Isaiah says that the servant "shall . . . sprinkle many nations," using a term that

---

18. Oswalt, *Isaiah, Chapters 40–66*, 111.

appears in Leviticus 16:14 to refer to the high priest sprinkling sacrificial blood on the altar to make atonement for his sin. The sprinkling in Isaiah 52:15, therefore, is probably a reference to the atoning death of the servant that Isaiah describes later in the passage (53:4–12).[19] If this is right, it is likely that Isaiah meant to include the "many nations" he mentions in 52:15 among the "many" for whom the servant's substitutionary death atones (53:12). Isaiah fills out this theme at the end of this section of the book as he describes a future pilgrimage of foreigners to God's "holy mountain" (56:1–7), where his temple will become "a house of prayer for all peoples" and where the nations will worship God together with Israel (56:7–8).

The Covenant of the Lord and the Servant of the Lord

In Isaiah's sixth major cycle of judgment and blessing (Isa. 56:9–62:12), the Lord's patience with injustice in Israel has run out. Israel is observing its traditional religious rituals but failing to follow the Lord's instruction to give freedom to the oppressed, to provide for the poor, to rest on the Sabbath, or to render justice and speak truthfully in their courts (58:1–59:15a). As the Lord looks across this landscape, he can find "no justice" and "no one to intercede" (59:15b–16). So he takes action himself, putting on the armor of salvation, righteousness, vengeance, and zeal (59:17). He repays the wicked for their evil deeds (59:18–19) and becomes a Redeemer to any who will turn from their transgression (59:20).

At the end of this passage, the Lord makes a "covenant"—a solemn agreement—with his people. He will give to them an individual on whom his Spirit will rest, who will ensure that the Lord's teaching continues forever (59:21). Earlier, Isaiah had referred to the servant who would complete Israel's mission to establish "justice in the

---

19. House, *Isaiah*, 2:489.

earth," bring the law to the distant "coastlands," and be "a light for
the nations" (42:4, 6; 49:6) as someone on whom God's Spirit would
rest (42:1) and who would be "a covenant for/to the people" (42:6;
49:8). The individual addressed here in 59:21, then, is likely to be
that same servant.[20]

New Heavens and a New Earth

Isaiah concludes his book with a seventh series of contrasts between
the eventual destruction that will come to those who have rejected
God and the blessing that will come to God's faithful servants (Isa.
65:1–66:24). After God's merciful delay, judgment will eventually
come (65:1–7). The faithful remnant within God's people will experience much hardship as this judgment takes place (65:8–12).[21] Finally,
however, God will separate his faithful servants from the faithless
(65:13–16), and God's servants will inhabit a new creation:

> For behold, I create new heavens
>   and a new earth,
> and the former things shall not be remembered
>   or come into mind.
> But be glad and rejoice forever
>   in that which I create;
> for behold, I created Jerusalem to be a joy,
>   and her people to be a gladness. (65:17–18)

The threefold use of the verb "create" here, especially with "heavens"
and "earth" as its object, recalls Genesis 1:1. It is a verb that Isaiah has
used frequently to describe God's creation of various features of the
natural world (e.g., Isa. 4:5; 40:26, 28; 42:5; 45:7).[22]

---

20. House, *Isaiah*, 2:604–5.
21. House, *Isaiah*, 2:702.
22. Koehler and Baumgartner, *Hebrew and Aramaic Lexicon*, 1:153–54.

This new creation will contain no weeping or distress (65:19). Life will last an unnaturally long time (65:20). People will build, plant, reap, and bear children in peace (65:21–23). Just as in 11:6–9, peace will reign in the animal world, and the serpent, whose insidious cleverness helped destroy the peace of the garden of Eden, will stay in the dust where it belongs (65:25; cf. Gen. 3:14). This will be a period, moreover, when "all nations and tongues" gather to see God's glory (Isa. 66:18) and when the survivors of God's judgment on Israel travel to the far corners of the world to announce God's fame. As a result, people from "all the nations" will join faithful Israel as full members of God's people and as worshipers of the Lord (66:18–23).

Isaiah's Vision of the World's Restoration

Isaiah, then, envisions the pathway by which God will fulfill his promise to bless all the nations of the earth through Abraham. God will do this despite Israel's failure to rise above the level of the rest of fallen humanity in its trusting obedience to God. Israel, and all the disobedient peoples of the earth, will pass through a time of judgment for the violence, injustice, oppression, and idolatry that characterize their societies, but then God will bring to Israel a great servant-king from the line of David.

God's Spirit will be on this royal servant, and he will be the mediator of a covenant between God, Israel, and the nations of the earth. He will be wise, just, and compassionate. His servanthood will extend to the point that, although totally innocent of wrongdoing himself, he will die for the sins of both Israel and the nations. He will embody Israel's vocation (cf. Ex. 19:5–6), bringing the light of God's teaching to the nations and calling all, whether within Israel or the nations, to turn from their transgression. Eventually, under his reign, God will restore all creation to the security, peace, and abundance of the garden in Eden, and God himself will be present there with his human creation.

The Coming of the Great Davidic King in Jeremiah and Ezekiel

Many of these same themes reappear in the prophets Jeremiah and Ezekiel in the late seventh and early sixth centuries BC. Jeremiah writes after Judah's idolatry and injustice have reached a low point under King Manasseh, who does "more evil than the nations had done whom the LORD destroyed before the people of Israel" (2 Kings 21:9). In a statement reminiscent of Isaiah 59:1–15, Jeremiah says that "the sin of Judah is written with a pen of iron; with a point of diamond it is engraved on the tablet of their heart" (Jer. 17:1). Judah, moreover, has suffered bitterly for its rebellion against God. Its cities lay in ruins, and much of its population has been exiled to Babylon (2 Kings 24:10–25:26).

Nevertheless, Jeremiah prophesies that God will one day replace the wicked "shepherds" over his people who have "scattered" the Lord's flock and "driven them away" (Jer. 23:2) with "shepherds over them who will care for them, and they shall fear no more, nor be dismayed, neither shall any be missing" (23:4). This will happen when the Lord "raise[s] up for David a righteous Branch, and he shall reign as king and deal wisely, and shall execute justice and righteousness in the land" (23:5). The Lord will "restore the fortunes of [his] people, Israel and Judah, . . . and . . . bring them back to the land that [he] gave to their fathers" (30:3). They will "serve the LORD their God and David their king," whom the Lord will "raise up for them" (30:9). He will "make a new covenant with the house of Israel and the house of Judah," unlike the previous covenant he made with them when he rescued them from slavery in Egypt (31:31–32). God will establish this new covenant with them by putting his law "within them" and writing it "on their hearts" (31:33). He will "forgive their iniquity" and "remember their sin no more" (31:34).

Ezekiel, from his home with the exiles in Babylon, similarly envisions a time when God will send to the exiled "sheep" of Israel a new and different shepherd, unlike the shepherd-kings who have exploited God's sheep and failed to take care of them, resulting in their dispersion "over all the mountains and on every high hill" (Ezek. 34:6; cf. 34:1–22):

> I will set up over them one shepherd, my servant David, and he shall feed them: he shall feed them and be their shepherd. And I, the LORD, will be their God, and my servant David shall be prince among them. (34:23–24)

Ezekiel says that during this time God will "make . . . a covenant of peace" with Israel (34:25), and his description of life under this covenant recalls the security and abundance of the garden of Eden. The Lord will "banish wild beasts from the land" (34:25). The woods, formerly feared, will now become a place of "blessing" where people go to sleep (34:26). Trees will yield fruit, the earth will produce crops, God's people will no longer be prey for the nations around them or the wild animals in their midst (34:27–28). They will know neither hunger nor shame, and just as in the garden of Eden, God will dwell "with them" (34:29–31). God will breathe new life into their dead bones (37:1–10), just as he had given the first man the breath of life (Gen. 2:7). He will, he says to his people, "put my Spirit within you, and you shall live" (Ezek. 37:14).

Conclusion

Isaiah, Jeremiah, and Ezekiel describe this great king in ambiguous ways. Although he appears to be a merciful answer to the judgments God has brought on his people in the eighth, seventh, and sixth centuries BC, the dimensions of his reign seem exaggerated for their own times. He will bring warfare to an end (Isa. 9:5; 11:6–9) and will rule with peace, justice, and righteousness forever (9:7; 11:4–5; cf. 32:1–8) in an idyllic setting of abundance and security (11:6–9). There are hints, moreover, that somehow this Davidic king is God himself. Among his many names are ones that mean "God is with us" (Isa. 7:14), "Mighty God" (9:6), and "The LORD is our righteousness" (Jer. 23:6). In Ezekiel, God at first says that he will personally search for his scattered sheep, reunite them, and feed them (Ezek. 34:11–16), and then that he will set up David his servant over them as their shepherd—"he shall feed them and be their shepherd" (34:23). Will God tend his sheep, or will a human king from David's descendants?[23] Matthew's Gospel answers this question.

---

23. Thanks to N. T. Wright for this insight during an undergraduate supervision in Downing College, Cambridge, in 1981.

3

The Great King and
Humble Servant Comes

Matthew begins his account of Jesus in a way that telegraphs to the reader, "This is a story of momentous importance!" The first words of his narrative have no verb, and this makes it look like a heading, or even a title for the narrative that follows: "The book of the genealogy of Jesus Christ, the son of David, the son of Abraham" (Matt. 1:1).[1] Matthew was writing in Greek, and his title echoes the two occurrences of the phrase "This is the book of the origin of . . ." in the Greek version of Genesis, a version he would have known (Gen. 2:4; 5:1 NETS).[2] The first occurrence of the phrase opens the part of Genesis that gives an account of the decline of creation into violence and chaos after the first man and woman disobeyed God: "This is the book of the origin of heaven and earth" (2:4 NETS). The other use of the phrase occurs in the statement "This is the book of the origin of human beings" (5:1 NETS). Matthew seems to be saying, therefore,

---

1. W. D. Davies and Dale C. Allison Jr., *The Gospel according to Saint Matthew*, International Critical Commentary, 3 vols. (London: T&T Clark, 1988–1997), 1:149–54.
2. Davies and Allison, *Matthew*, 1:150.

that he is about to tell a story that parallels in its importance the stories of creation (cf. Gen. 2:4) and the origin of Adam and his descendants (cf. 5:1). This story concerns the coming of the great Davidic king and humble servant of the Lord whom Isaiah, Jeremiah, and Ezekiel expected and who would fulfill God's promises to Abraham.

The Great Davidic King Has Come

Matthew loses no time informing his readers that a man named Jesus is this great king, and as his Gospel proceeds, he shows repeatedly and in various ways that Jesus fits the prophetic profile for who this king would be. His crucial first line claims that Jesus is the "Christ," a term that in its Greek form simply means "anointed" but in a Jewish context refers to the Israelite ceremony of anointing a person with oil in order to designate that person as king (1 Sam. 9:16; 10:1; 16:3, 13). The Israelite king, then, can simply be called the Lord's "Anointed," or the Lord's "Christ" (Ps. 2:2), and Matthew begins his Gospel by telling us that Jesus is the anointed king in the line of David whom the prophets expected to come.

The genealogy that follows Matthew's first line revolves around David, as Matthew 1:17 shows: "So all the generations from Abraham to David were fourteen generations, and from David to the deportation to Babylon fourteen generations, and from the deportation to Babylon to the Christ fourteen generations." In other words, there is a direct historical line from Abraham to Jesus Christ that runs right through the great king David.

Matthew also wants his readers to know that Jesus is born in Bethlehem, the ancestral home of David (1 Sam. 16:1, 4). At the time of Jesus's birth, Matthew says, scholars were expecting the anointed one of David's lineage to come from precisely that town, in accord with the prophecy of Micah 5:2 that a ruler will come from there to "shepherd" Israel (Matt. 2:3–6).

Although Jesus is born in Bethlehem in Judea, in the south of Israel, Matthew tells us that his family, and Jesus himself, eventually settles in Galilee, in the north of Israel. Matthew wants to make sure his readers know that this movement fulfills Isaiah's prophecy that "the land of Zebulun and the land of Naphtali," also called "Galilee of the Gentiles" and populated by "people dwelling in darkness," will see "a great light," brought by a royal descendant of David who will rule in wisdom and bring peace, justice, and righteousness to the region (Matt. 4:15–16; cf. Isa. 9:1–7). Jesus goes "throughout all Galilee, teaching in their synagogues and proclaiming the gospel of the kingdom and healing every disease and every affliction among the people" (Matt. 4:23). The great Davidic king has come and is proclaiming the establishment of the kingdom of justice, safety, peace, and security that Isaiah describes in Isaiah 9:1–7; 11:1–16; and 32:1–8.

According to Isaiah, the "root of Jesse" will gather exiled Israelites of both the northern and southern kingdoms back to their homeland (Isa. 11:11–13), so Matthew adds this:

> [Jesus's] fame spread throughout all Syria, and they brought him all the sick, those afflicted with various diseases and pains, those oppressed by demons, those having seizures, and paralytics, and he healed them. And great crowds followed him from Galilee and the Decapolis, and from Jerusalem and Judea, and from beyond the Jordan. (Matt. 4:24–25)

Matthew paints a picture here of people from all over the Israelite kingdom as it existed in its united form under King David and from regions dominated by Gentiles (Syria, the Decapolis, the Nabatean kingdom beyond the Jordan) coming to where Jesus is in Galilee, hearing his teaching and receiving his healing. Matthew does not say so explicitly, but his description makes it seem as if "a highway" exists "from Assyria . . . , as there was for Israel when they came up out of the land of Egypt" (Isa. 11:16). The second and greater exodus has begun (cf. Jer. 23:5–8).

Directly after this summary of Jesus's teaching and healing ministry, Matthew provides both a long sample of Jesus's teaching (Matt. 5:1–7:29) and a lengthy narrative describing the sort of healing that Jesus performs (8:1–9:34). His description of Jesus's teaching (the so-called Sermon on the Mount) is reminiscent of Isaiah's description of the divine wisdom and effective teaching of the coming Davidic king (Isa. 9:6; 11:2; 32:1–4). "Do not think that I have come to abolish the Law or the Prophets," Jesus says; "I have not come to abolish them but to fulfill them" (Matt. 5:17). He then takes representative samples of the Mosaic law and moves them to the end of the trajectory toward which they were already pointing.[3] The Mosaic law forbids murder and adultery, regulates divorce with a legal certificate, forbids oath breaking and overretaliation for an injury, and commands love for neighbor. Jesus, however, forbids the angry and lustful thoughts that lead to murder and adultery, allows for divorce only in cases of sexual immorality, insists that people always keep their simple word without oath taking, forbids any form of retaliation, and urges people to love not merely their neighbors but also their enemies (5:21–48).

The Mosaic law was perfectly designed as a sensible and compassionate body of legislation for an ancient Near Eastern nation that included within it people who wanted to follow God's will from the heart as well as those who were in total rebellion against God, and everyone in between. Jesus, however, is providing instruction for those who want to begin living in the present in ways that will become second nature when his peaceful kingdom is fully established.

---

3. For more on this, see Frank Thielman, *The Law and the New Testament: The Question of Continuity*, Companions to the New Testament (New York: Crossroad, 1999), 49–58, and the literature cited on 73n6.

The rest of this section of Jesus's teaching emphasizes the importance of living from a sincere desire to please God. It is as if those who seek to live in the way Jesus describes have started to experience a reversal of Genesis 6:5. Rather than "every intention of the thoughts" of their hearts being "only evil," those who follow Jesus's teaching act out of a sincere, heartfelt desire to please God. They give to the needy, pray, and fast not in public ways for the recognition they will receive but privately and sincerely (Matt. 6:1–18). They trust God, rather than money and possessions, to meet their needs (6:19–34). They do not point out what is wrong with others as an evasion tactic for dealing with their own faults (7:1–6). They treat others as they want to be treated (7:12). They are like trees that bear good fruit: their good conduct matches the transformed heart that is within them (7:15–23).

Matthew says that when Jesus finishes teaching all this, the crowds are "astonished . . . , for he was teaching them as one who had authority, and not as their scribes" (7:28–29). The work of the scribes of Jesus's time was to interpret and apply the Mosaic law, but Jesus authoritatively proclaims a new law. His demeanor, then, is fully compatible with the wise, royal ruler of Isaiah 11:1–16.

Matthew next describes Jesus's healing activity, and here, too, the reader of his Gospel who is familiar with Isaiah can easily see a resemblance between Jesus's ministry and the peace, security, abundance, and restoration to fellowship with God that will characterize the renewal Isaiah had prophesied. Jesus cures a Jewish man of leprosy (Matt. 8:1–4), a Roman centurion's servant of paralysis (8:5–13), and a disciple's relative of a fever (8:14–15). When he and his disciples are caught in a storm on the Sea of Galilee and his disciples are afraid of perishing, he rebukes the winds and the sea and produces "a great calm" (8:26). It is as if the Creator has restored peace to his creation, just as he does in Psalm 107:23–32. The "Mighty God" and

"Prince of Peace" of Isaiah 9:6 is bringing God's presence and peace to his people.

Jesus then forgives the sins of another paralyzed man and afterward heals him (Matt. 9:1–8). He banquets with, and offers mercy to, outcasts and sinners (9:9–13). He raises a little girl from the dead (9:18–26). The day is beginning to dawn in which the Lord "will swallow up death forever" and "will wipe away tears from all faces" (Isa. 25:8), when he will provide "a hiding place from the wind, a shelter from the storm" (32:2), when his servant will open the eyes of the blind—whether physically or spiritually—and set people free who are in bondage to sin (42:7; 61:1).

At the end of this section of Matthew's narrative, two blind men follow Jesus, shouting, "Have mercy on us, Son of David," and he heals them (Matt. 9:27–29). A few sentences later, as if to end this long section of Jesus's teaching and healing activity in the same way that it began, Matthew says once again (cf. 4:23) that Jesus "went throughout all the cities and villages, teaching in their synagogues and proclaiming the gospel of the kingdom and healing every disease and every affliction" (9:35).[4]

Now, however, Matthew adds to this summary: "When he saw the crowds, he had compassion for them, because they were harassed and helpless, like sheep without a shepherd" (9:36). Matthew makes clear that in his teaching and healing ministry, Jesus acts as the Davidic shepherd-king of Ezekiel 34:23–24 (cf. Num. 27:17; Jer. 23:1–6). He rescues his weary, abused sheep, gathering them together so that he can feed and tend them.

The Great Davidic King and the Nations

Directly after this passage, Matthew describes how Jesus comments that "the harvest is plentiful, but the laborers are few" (Matt. 9:37)

---

4. Cf. Davies and Allison, *Matthew*, 2:146.

and how he then chooses twelve disciples whom he sends out and instructs to "go nowhere among the Gentiles and enter no town of the Samaritans" but instead to go to "the lost sheep of the house of Israel" (10:5–6). At first, this seems to contradict the emphasis in the Prophets, and especially in Isaiah, on the inclusion of the nations in the restoration of God's people and in the new creation. Did not Isaiah say that the great king would "stand as a signal for the peoples" and that "the nations [would] inquire" of him (Isa. 11:10; cf. 11:12)? Would not the Lord's servant both "raise up" a united Israel and become "a light for the nations" so that God's "salvation may reach to the end of the earth" (49:6)?

Isaiah, however, seems to envision a certain order for the renewal of the peoples of the earth. God will first gather the remnant of his people Israel, and then the nations will come to the restored Israel. In Isaiah 2:1–5, the prophet assumes that "in the latter days," the people of Judah and Jerusalem will walk so completely in the path of the Lord's teaching that "all the nations" will look up to Mount Zion and say,

> Come, let us go up to the mountain of the LORD,
>   to the house of the God of Jacob,
> that he may teach us his ways
>   and that we may walk in his paths. (2:3)

Later in Isaiah,

> The Lord GOD,
>   who gathers the outcasts of Israel, declares,
> "I will gather yet others to him
>   besides those already gathered." (56:8; cf. 2:1–5; Zech. 8:23)

Matthew wants us to know that although there were anticipatory indications of the servant-king's outreach to the nations (e.g.,

Matt. 8:5–13; 15:21–28), Jesus first assembles a group of followers who represent the faithful remnant of Israel.[5] The number twelve for Jesus's inner group of disciples is significant. It corresponds to the twelve tribes of Israel and indicates that Jesus considers his followers to be the faithful remnant of Israel in whom God will begin the renewal of the earth. At one point in his narrative, he tells these twelve disciples that "in the new world" they will sit beside his glorious throne on twelve thrones of their own, "judging the twelve tribes of Israel" (19:28).

The mission of the twelve to proclaim the soon-coming kingdom and to "heal the sick, raise the dead, cleanse lepers, [and] cast out demons" brings the reign of Jesus to Israel itself and calls on Israelites throughout the land to respond to the good news that, in Jesus, God has brought the world closer to the period of peace and security that the prophets had foretold (10:7–8). It becomes clear from the instructions Jesus gives to his twelve disciples, however, that many Israelites will reject their message and the rule of the great Davidic king. "They will deliver you over to courts," Jesus warns them, "and flog you in their synagogues, and you will be dragged before governors and kings for my sake, to bear witness before them and the Gentiles" (10:17–18). It is this rejection of Jesus that most clearly indicates the correspondence between Jesus and the humble servant that Isaiah described.

The Great King as Suffering Servant

Matthew 11 opens with a description of John the Baptist's suffering and discouragement in prison. John is the last of the prophets (Matt. 11:13), and before his imprisonment, he pointed to Jesus's work as the fulfillment of Isaiah's prophecy of Israel's restoration (3:1–12; cf. Isa.

---

5. On this, see Davies and Allison, *Matthew*, 2:151–52.

40:3). Now, however, in a moment of doubt, John has sent a message to Jesus with the question "Are you the one who is to come, or shall we look for another?" (Matt. 11:3). Jesus sends this message back:

> The blind receive their sight and the lame walk, lepers are cleansed and the deaf hear, and the dead are raised up, and the poor have good news preached to them. And blessed is the one who is not offended by me. (11:5–6)

Jesus is echoing here the description of the Lord's servant in Isaiah 61:1:

> The Spirit of the Lord GOD is upon me,
> > because the LORD has anointed me
> to bring good news to the poor;
> > he has sent me to bind up the brokenhearted,
> to proclaim liberty to the captives,
> > and the opening of the prison to those who are bound.

John's first conviction about Jesus was correct: he is the servant of whom Isaiah prophesied, and he has brought with him the dawning of the day of Israel's, and the earth's, restoration.

Although this is true, the imprisonment of John the Baptist casts a dark shadow over Jesus's own ministry. If John is God's prophet and has been imprisoned, what will happen to Jesus, the servant of the Lord?

As Matthew's narrative progresses, opposition to Jesus among the elite classes in Judean society intensifies, and readers begin to suspect that something like what happened to John is in store for Jesus.[6] He

---

6. Jesus had already dangerously provoked the "scribes"—the scholars who applied the Mosaic law to everyday life—when he forgave the sins of the paralyzed man. Assuming that by forgiving sins Jesus was doing something only God could do, they commented, "This man is blaspheming" (Matt. 9:3). The penalty in the Mosaic law for blasphemy was death by stoning (Lev. 24:16, 23; John 10:33).

allows his disciples to pick and eat grain, and he heals a man's crippled hand—both on the Sabbath day (Matt. 12:1–14). Each of these activities provoke the Pharisees, a group in the Judaism of the time who are particularly meticulous interpreters of the Mosaic law (Acts 26:5). They believe that Jesus is permitting and engaging in work on the Sabbath, and the penalty for that, according to the Mosaic law, is death by stoning (Ex. 31:14; 35:2; Num. 15:32, 35). It is no surprise, then, that in response to Jesus's activity on the Sabbath, "the Pharisees [go] out and [conspire] against him, how to destroy him" (Matt. 12:14).

Matthew's introduction and conclusion to these two stories of conflict on the Sabbath recall the humility and peaceful nature of the Lord's servant in Isaiah 42:1–9. Immediately before the two stories, Jesus says this to his disciples:

> Come to me, all who labor and are heavy laden, and I will give you rest. Take my yoke upon you, and learn from me, for I am gentle and lowly in heart, and you will find rest for your souls. For my yoke is easy and my burden is light. (Matt. 11:28–30)

Both Jesus's willingness to allow his disciples to pick and eat grain on the Sabbath and his healing of a man with a crippled hand on the Sabbath put this principle into effect. He relieves the burdens of his hungry disciples and the disabled man on God's day of rest. He does not flippantly disregard God's command to avoid work on the Sabbath, but as with his approach to the Mosaic law elsewhere, he authoritatively fulfills it in a new way that is consistent with its deepest meaning. What better way to honor the day on which God rested at the end of creation than by using it to help remake creation as a place of abundant provision and security, free from hunger and sickness?

Immediately after these two accounts, Matthew says that when Jesus learns of the Pharisees' plot to kill him, he withdraws and carries on his healing ministry more quietly elsewhere (12:15–16). Matthew then says that Jesus does this to "fulfill what was spoken by the prophet Isaiah" (Matt. 12:17), and he quotes Isaiah 42:1–3:

> Behold, my servant whom I have chosen,
>> my beloved with whom my soul is well pleased.
> I will put my Spirit upon him,
>> and he will proclaim justice to the Gentiles.
> He will not quarrel or cry aloud,
>> nor will anyone hear his voice in the streets;
> a bruised reed he will not break,
>> and a smoldering wick he will not quench,
> until he brings justice to victory;
>> and in his name the Gentiles will hope.
>> (Matt. 12:18–21)

Like the servant in Isaiah 42, Jesus does not respond to the Pharisees' opposition with angry debates or violent protests. He does not look for his opponents' vulnerabilities and take advantage of them to mount a counterattack. Rather, he gently and patiently keeps working toward a society and a world in which what is right will prevail, in which there will be no more hunger, sickness, or miscarriage of justice.

The Atoning Death of the Servant and the Establishment of the New Covenant

Matthew maintains that in Jesus, the light of that world has dawned. It certainly has not fully arrived, however, and this is never clearer than in the miscarriage of justice that leads to the death of Jesus, the servant and king. As Jesus's teaching and healing ministry continues in Matthew's story, the opposition to Jesus from some of the

Pharisees grows stronger, and its root cause also becomes clear. Immediately after Matthew quotes Isaiah 42:1–3, for example, Jesus heals a demon-oppressed man who is both blind and mute (Matt. 12:22), but the Pharisees respond to this healing by claiming that Jesus can control demons only because he is allied with them (12:24). Jesus's answer to this charge includes an analogy between his opponents and a fruit-bearing tree:

> Either make the tree good and its fruit good, or make the tree bad and its fruit bad, for the tree is known by its fruit. You brood of vipers! How can you speak good, when you are evil? For out of the abundance of the heart the mouth speaks. (12:33–34; cf. 7:15–20)

The Pharisees who oppose Jesus have a heart problem. Like all humanity in Genesis 6:5, "every intention of the thoughts of [their] heart" is "only evil continually," and just as with Israel's leadership in Jeremiah's time, their sin is "written with a pen of iron; with a point of diamond it is engraved on the tablet of their heart" (Jer. 17:1). As Jeremiah recognized, this is a problem that only God can correct, by writing his teaching "on their hearts" (31:33; cf. Deut. 30:6), but at least for now, Israel's leadership, like its leadership in the times of Isaiah, will "keep on hearing, but . . . not understand" and "keep on seeing, but . . . not perceive" what God is doing among them through Jesus, the great Davidic king (Isa. 6:9; cf. Matt. 13:13–15).

Eventually, Jesus tells his disciples, this obtuseness to the real significance of who he is and what he came to do will lead some of the elites of Judean society to plot his death (16:21; 17:12, 22). His death will not merely be a miscarriage of justice but will be the fulfillment of his vocation: "not to be served but to serve, and to give his life as a ransom for many" (20:28). Like the servant of the Lord in Isaiah

53:11–12, Jesus will bear "the sin of many" and make "intercession for the transgressors."

The prophecies of Isaiah about the servant, and of Jesus about himself, are finally realized when Jesus travels to Jerusalem with his disciples for the annual Jewish festival of Passover. Passover was normally a joyful time when many Jewish people traveled from their homes, sometimes in distant lands, to Jerusalem to celebrate God's rescue of his people from slavery in Egypt at the time of the exodus. As Jesus enters Jerusalem early in the week during which the day of Passover fell, many people in the crowds who have come to the city begin to acclaim him "the Son of David" (Matt. 21:9). Amid their shouts, Jesus comes to the temple, the magnificent building that is the physical center of Jewish worship in Jesus's time.

There Jesus criticizes the Jewish leadership in Jerusalem for turning the temple into a profitable business for themselves at the expense of often poor worshipers.[7] "It is written," Jesus says, "'My house shall be called a house of prayer,' but you make it a den of robbers" (21:13). He is quoting Isaiah, who prophesied that one day "foreigners" would "join themselves to the LORD, / to minister to him, to love the name of the LORD, / and to be his servants" (Isa. 56:6) and also prophesied that his "house [would] be called a house of prayer for all people" (56:7).[8] By basing his criticism of temple operations on this passage, and by healing "the blind and the lame" who come "to him in the temple" (Matt. 21:14), Jesus is signaling that he intends to usher in the time of Israel's (and the world's) renewal. Isaiah had prophesied that one day

---

7. On this point, see Grant R. Osborne, *Matthew*, Zondervan Exegetical Commentary on the New Testament (Grand Rapids, MI: Zondervan, 2010), 762.

8. Jesus's reference to making the temple a "den of robbers" echoes Jer. 7:11, where the prophet criticizes Judah for thinking that they can break God's most basic commands and then depend on the presence of the temple in their midst magically to shield them from God's judgment. See J. A. Thompson, *The Book of Jeremiah*, New International Commentary on the Old Testament (Grand Rapids, MI: Eerdmans, 1980), 280–81.

> the eyes of the blind shall be opened,
>> and the ears of the deaf unstopped;
> then the lame man shall leap like a deer,
>> and the tongue of the mute sing for joy. (Isa. 35:5–6;
>>> cf. 29:18–19)

The wealthy and politically powerful temple hierarchy—the "chief priests"—are profiting from the status quo and do not welcome the radical social changes that Jesus's recollection of Isaiah implies. Not surprisingly, then, they join Jesus's old antagonists, the scribes and the Pharisees, in opposition to him.

In response to their opposition, Jesus tells a parable reminiscent of the parable of the unfruitful vineyard in Isaiah 5:1–7. In Jesus's version, the chief priests and the Pharisees are clearly cast as the responsible party in the failure of God's vineyard to yield the fruit that God required of it in harvest time (Matt. 21:33–46). There is no room in their political or theological framework for a Davidic king of this sort, and so they "[seek] to arrest him" (21:46). Eventually, they "[gather] in the palace of the high priest, whose name was Caiaphas, and [plot] together in order to arrest Jesus by stealth and kill him" (26:3–4).

Since Jesus knows this is coming (26:2), he now makes clear to his disciples that what is about to take place will fulfill the expectations of the prophets Isaiah and Jeremiah for the establishment of a new covenant. Isaiah had described the Lord's servant as someone who would be

> a covenant for the people,
>> a light for the nations,
>> to open the eyes that are blind,
> to bring out the prisoners from the dungeon,

from the prison those who sit in darkness. (Isa. 42:6–7; cf. 49:8; 59:21)

Jeremiah had envisioned the beginning of Israel's renewed relationship with God as God's establishment of "a new covenant with the house of Israel and the house of Judah" (Jer. 31:31). God's people would not break this new covenant, as they broke the Mosaic covenant at the time of the exodus. Rather, this time, God would "put [his] law within them" and would "write it on their hearts" (Jer. 31:33). Jesus uses the celebration of the Passover meal with his disciples to recall these passages and to teach them that his death marks the beginning of this new covenant:

> Now as they were eating, Jesus took bread, and after blessing it broke it and gave it to the disciples, and said, "Take, eat; this is my body." And he took a cup, and when he had given thanks he gave it to them, saying, "Drink of it, all of you, for this is my blood of the covenant, which is poured out for many for the forgiveness of sins. I tell you I will not drink again of this fruit of the vine until that day when I drink it new with you in my Father's kingdom." (Matt. 26:26–29)

Jesus's statement that his blood, which will establish this covenant, will be "poured out for many for the forgiveness of sins" recalls Isaiah's description of the Lord's servant as one who was "pierced for our transgressions," "crushed for our iniquities," "stricken for the transgression of [God's] people," who will "make many to be accounted righteous," and who "bore the sin of many" (Isa. 53:5, 8, 11, 12). As Jesus goes through his arrest and trial, moreover, he is aware that what is taking place and his own response to the painful events he is experiencing are fulfillments of Isaiah's prophecies concerning the Lord's servant (Matt. 26:54, 56). Just as the servant "opened not his mouth" when he was mistreated but was "silent" (Isa. 53:7), so Jesus remains "silent" during much of his sham trial before the high priest, the scribes, and the people's council (Matt. 26:63). Twice Matthew says that Jesus gives "no answer" to the Roman governor Pilate when asked whether the council's serious charges against him of political sedition are correct (27:11–14). Just as the servant was reckoned to be wicked "although he had done no violence, / and there was no deceit in his mouth" (Isa. 53:9), so even Pilate's wife recognizes that Jesus is an "innocent man" (Matt. 27:19 NIV).

After Jesus is falsely convicted, Pilate has him scourged and crucified (27:26), punishments reminiscent of Isaiah's statement that the servant "was pierced" and experienced "chastisement" and "wounds" for the transgressions and iniquities of others (Isa. 53:5). After his death, Jesus is buried in a tomb owned by "a rich man from Arimathea, named Joseph, who also [is] a disciple of Jesus" (Matt. 27:57). This is not an exact match with Isaiah's statement that "they made [the servant's] grave with the wicked / and with a rich man in his death" (Isa. 53:9), but it is both close enough to be reminiscent of Isaiah and different enough to allay suspicion that Matthew was managing the story of Jesus to match Isaiah's account of the servant.

The Defeat of Death and the Inclusion of the Nations

In Isaiah, however, the death of the servant is not the end of his life. According to Isaiah 53:10,

> When his soul makes an offering for guilt,
>   he shall see his offspring; he shall prolong his days;
>   the will of the LORD shall prosper in his hand.

As Paul House comments, the animals sacrificed as guilt offerings all died, but the servant continues to live and prosper after he has died as a guilt offering. The most reasonable explanation of this, House says, is that the promises made in Isaiah 25:6–12 and 26:19 will be fulfilled. One day, the Lord will

> swallow up . . .
>> the covering that is cast over all peoples,
>> the veil that is spread over all nations.
> He will swallow up death forever;
>> and the Lord GOD will wipe away tears from all faces.
>> (25:7–8)

One day, the Lord tells his people,

> Your dead shall live; their bodies shall rise.
>> You who dwell in the dust, awake and sing for joy!
> For your dew is a dew of light,
>> and the earth will give birth to the dead. (26:19)[9]

So, it seems, after the sacrificial death of the Lord's servant, he will be the first to experience the fulfillment of these promises. It is not surprising, then, that Matthew ends his Gospel with an account of Jesus's resurrection from the dead (28:1–15).

In Isaiah, the servant does not simply rise from the dead for his own benefit. The prophet says that he will have "offspring" (Isa. 53:10) and, at least in the Greek version of Isaiah, that he will "inherit many" (53:12 NETS).[10] As we saw in chapter 2, moreover, it is likely that Isaiah's reference to "many" here echoes his reference to the "many nations" in 52:15 that the servant will "sprinkle" with

---

9. Paul R. House, *Isaiah*, Mentor Commentary, 2 vols. (Fearn, Ross-shire, Scotland: Mentor, 2019), 2:503–4. See also the discussion in N. T. Wright, *The Resurrection of the Son of God*, vol. 3 of *Christian Origins and the Question of God* (Minneapolis: Fortress, 2003), 115–18.

10. See also the translation of the Hebrew text in House, *Isaiah*, 2:505–6, "Therefore, I will divide to him the many as a portion," and the translation of the NAB, "Therefore I will give him his portion among the many."

sacrificial blood. Isaiah's servant gathers his "offspring" and his inheritance of many people, therefore, from all the nations of the earth. The servant's resurrection, moreover, signals the beginning of the removal of the veil of death from his offspring.

If we now look back over Matthew's story with the inclusion of the nations and the defeat of death in mind, it is easy to see that he has foreshadowed this development throughout his narrative. When at the beginning of the story the "wise men from the east" come to Jerusalem seeking to present offerings to the "king of the Jews" (Matt. 2:1–2, 11), we can sense the fulfillment of Isaiah 2:1–5:

> Many peoples shall come, and say:
> "Come, let us go up to the mountain of the LORD,
>   to the house of the God of Jacob,
> that he may teach us his ways
>   and that we may walk in his paths." (2:3)[11]

As the story progresses (as already noted), Jesus restricts his and his disciples' work mainly to Israel, but even in this phase, he heals a Roman centurion's servant (Matt. 8:5–13) and the daughter of a non-Israelite woman who lived outside the land of Israel (15:21–28), strongly commending the faith of both (8:10; 15:28). "Many will come from east and west and recline at table with Abraham, Isaac, and Jacob in the kingdom of heaven" (8:11), Jesus tells his followers after healing the Roman centurion's servant.

His criticism of the temple authorities, moreover, focuses on reminding them of Isaiah 56:7, a statement from a longer passage in Isaiah (56:1–8) that describes how, when the Lord's restoration of Israel comes, it will include "the foreigner" (56:3, 6), and God's temple will become "a house of prayer for all peoples" (56:7). It is true that

---

11. Cf. Osborne, *Matthew*, 86.

when Jesus quotes Isaiah 56:7 in Matthew 21:13, he does not include the phrase "for all peoples," but Matthew probably counted on his readers to know the passage well and therefore to understand the important role that the inclusion of the nations in God's purposes played in it.[12]

Matthew has also hinted that with the coming of Jesus, the removal of the curse of death for the restored people of God has begun. Thus, when a "ruler" comes and kneels before Jesus and asks him to bring his daughter, who has just died, back to life, Jesus does it (Matt. 9:18–19, 23–26). When Jesus sends his twelve disciples out to proclaim the nearness of God's kingdom, he tells them not only to heal the sick, cleanse lepers, and cast out demons but also to "raise the dead" (10:8). At the time of Jesus's death, moreover, "the tombs also were opened. And many bodies of the saints who had fallen asleep were raised, and coming out of the tombs after his resurrection they went into the holy city and appeared to many" (27:52–53).[13]

Conclusion

It is fitting, then, that at end of his Gospel, Matthew tells us that the resurrected Jesus sends his disciples to "all nations" to make other disciples for Jesus, "baptizing them in the name of the Father and of the Son and of the Holy Spirit, teaching them to observe all that I have commanded you" (Matt. 28:19–20). The disciples of Jesus are the core of the restored Israel. Jesus has made a new covenant with them and set before them a new law that God will write on their hearts. This law has shown them how they should live as faithful followers of the humble servant-king.

---

12. Osborne correctly recognizes this point. *Matthew*, 762. Like Matthew, Luke 19:46 does not include the phrase, but it does appear in Mark 11:17.

13. According to Wright, "[Matthew] was not saying that this really was the great general resurrection; it was a strange semi-anticipation of it." *Resurrection*, 635.

Their vocation is now to gather God's people not only from Israel but from all the corners of the earth and to bring them, like the wise men, to Jesus and teach them his ways. The time of Israel's restoration has dawned, and the vise grip of death on God's human creatures since the time of Adam and Eve has been loosened. The restoration of humanity to what God created it to be has begun with the formation, in Jesus's followers, of the restored Israel that Isaiah envisioned. Eventually, through the faithfulness of Jesus's disciples to "make disciples of all nations," God's promise that Abraham would be God's instrument to bless "all the families of the earth" (Gen. 12:3) will be fulfilled, and Isaiah's vision that the nations would come to Mount Zion to learn the ways of the Lord will come to pass (Isa. 2:3).

Jesus's final sentence in the Gospel is the promise that he will "[be] with" his disciples "always, to the end of the age" (Matt. 28:20). This statement echoes Matthew's comment at the beginning of the Gospel that Jesus's coming will fulfill the prophecy in Isaiah 7:14. According to that promise, a virgin will bear a son who will be named "Immanuel," a name, Matthew tells his readers, that means "God with us" (Matt. 1:23).[14] The Gospel begins and ends, therefore, with the claim that in Jesus God is once again "with" his people, as he was in the garden of Eden and as he would be, according to Jeremiah and Ezekiel, in the time of Israel's restoration (Jer. 31:33; Ezek. 37:27; cf. Lev. 26:12).

---

14. Jesus's promise to "[be] with" his disciples also echoes his statement in Matt. 18:20, "For where two or three are gathered in my name, there am I among them." Davies and Allison, *Matthew*, 3:686.

4

The New Creation

Matthew's Gospel ends with Jesus's hopeful instructions to his disciples to "go . . . and make disciples of all nations" (Matt. 28:19) and with the promise that Jesus, like God himself in the garden of Eden, will be with his disciples as they carry out his commission. At this point in the story, however, Jesus's disciples are not fully transformed. Matthew specifies, for example, that the group of disciples to whom Jesus gives his commission numbers only eleven (28:16), a grim reminder that one of Jesus's inner circle of twelve, betrayed him: Judas facilitated his arrest and murder (26:14–16, 21, 25, 47–50).

Matthew also comments that when the eleven disciples see the resurrected Jesus in Galilee, right before he gives them their commission, they worship him, though some doubt (28:17). This, too, is a reminder that throughout the preceding narrative, the trust of the twelve disciples in Jesus has been somewhat defective. Five times Jesus has addressed one or more of them as people of "little faith" (6:30; 8:26; 14:31; 16:8; 17:20). Peter, the "rock" on which Jesus will build his church (16:18), has suffered a severe rebuke from Jesus for failing to understand that Jesus's mission involves suffering (16:23).

All the disciples fled at the time of Jesus's arrest (26:56), and while the council of Judean leaders was examining Jesus, Peter was outside in the high priest's courtyard vowing that he did "not know the man" (26:74).

What has happened to change this unpromising group of eleven disciples into the intrepid corps of twelve that will one day carry out Jesus's commission so faithfully that they will "be dragged before governors and kings for [his] sake" (10:18)? The book of Acts tells this story and reveals that the earliest Christians thought of themselves as the beginning of God's restoration of his people in the period of the new creation.

The Pilgrimage of Exiles to Zion in the Acts of the Apostles

The Acts of the Apostles is basically an account of how the Holy Spirit, the powerful and personal presence of God, transforms the earliest followers of Jesus into the restored people of God, the beginnings of God's new creation. "You will receive power," Jesus tells his disciples at the story's beginning, "when the Holy Spirit has come upon you, and you will be my witnesses in Jerusalem and in all Judea and Samaria, and to the ends of the earth" (Acts 1:8). Luke (the author of Acts) then describes how the Spirit guides and empowers the first Christians to carry out their mandate of gathering a new people of God composed not only of Israelites but also of people from the earth's many nations.[1]

Among the eleven disciples' first actions is the restoration of their number to twelve, the number of Israel's twelve tribes (Acts 1:13–26).[2] This indicates that they, and those who believe the good news

---

1. Luke refers to the Holy Spirit fifty-seven times and fairly evenly throughout his narrative. The only major swath of text without a reference to the Holy Spirit is Acts 21:12–28:24.

2. For a discussion of this act, see Joseph A. Fitzmyer, *The Acts of the Apostles: A New Translation with Introduction and Commentary*, Anchor Bible 31 (New York: Doubleday, 1998), 220–21.

about Jesus they proclaim, are the answer to the prophets' promise that God would rekindle his relationship with his people. Luke also wants his readers to know that the number of Christians gathered in Jerusalem at this time is "about 120" (1:15), ten times twelve. Here, then, is the core of the restored Israel.

It is on these 120 Christians in Jerusalem that the Holy Spirit comes "like a mighty rushing wind" (2:2). This description recalls the prophet Ezekiel's promise that God will one day restore the fortunes of defeated and exiled Israel by breathing life into the nation's dead bones, just as God breathed life into the first man (Gen. 2:7).[3] "Prophesy to the breath," the Lord tells Ezekiel, "prophesy, son of man, and say to the breath, Thus says the Lord GOD: Come from the four winds, O breath, and breathe on these slain, that they may live" (Ezek. 37:9). In the Greek translation of the Old Testament, the word that Luke uses for "wind" is the word that appears in Genesis for the life-giving "breath" of God, and the word for "breath" in Ezekiel is identical to the word that Luke uses for the Holy "Spirit." It seems likely that Luke is trying to communicate to his readers that the day of Israel's prophesied restoration has dawned.

Luke then tells his readers that the sound of the wind causes a crowd of Jewish pilgrims "from every nation under heaven" who have come to Jerusalem for the festival of Pentecost to "[come] together" (Acts 2:5–6). The apostle Peter uses this opportunity to explain to the crowd the significance of what is happening, the significance of Jesus as the great Davidic king promised in the Scriptures, the tragedy of his death, and the meaning of both his resurrection and his exaltation to a position of authority beside God in the present (2:14–36). Peter then calls on this international gathering of Jewish people to

---

3. See, e.g., F. F. Bruce, *The Book of the Acts*, rev. ed., New International Commentary on the New Testament (Grand Rapids, MI: Eerdmans, 1988), 50; Craig S. Keener, *Acts: An Exegetical Commentary*, 4 vols. (Grand Rapids, MI: Baker, 2012–2015), 1:798, 801–2.

"repent" of their previous rejection of what God is doing in their midst and "be baptized every one of you in the name of Jesus Christ for the forgiveness of your sins." When they do this, he tells them, they, too, "will receive the gift of the Holy Spirit" (2:38). Peter continues, "For the promise is for you and for your children and for all who are far off, everyone whom the Lord our God calls to himself" (2:39; cf. Isa. 2:1–3; Mic. 4:1–2). The story ends with the comment that "there were added that day about three thousand souls" (2:41).

By the end of this important day, then, God has started to fulfill such promises as Isaiah 11:12, which says that Israel's great Davidic king will one day "assemble the banished of Israel, / and gather the dispersed of Judah / from the four corners of the earth," and Jeremiah 23:3, where the Lord says, "I will gather the remnant of my flock out of all the countries where I have driven them, and I will bring them back to their fold, and they shall be fruitful and multiply."[4] Israelites scattered among many nations have converged on Mount Zion for the pilgrimage festival of Pentecost, and in a single day, the numbers of restored Israelites have increased to three thousand.

Luke next describes the character of this new community (Acts 2:42–47). They learn from the apostles, eat together, and pray. Amazing miracles happen among them, and they hold their property in common, "selling their possessions and belongings and distributing the proceeds to all, as any [have] need" (2:45). Later he says that because of this communitarian approach to their personal property, "there was not a needy person among them" (4:34). Luke emphasizes the joy that characterizes the group: "They received their food with glad and generous hearts, praising God and having favor with all the people" (2:46–47).

---

4. See also Isa. 49:11–12; Ezek. 34:11–16; Mic. 2:12; 4:6–8. On the theme of exiled Israel's ingathering, see especially Daniel I. Block, *The Book of Ezekiel, Chapters 25–48*, New International Commentary on the Old Testament (Grand Rapids, MI: Eerdmans, 1998), 290–91.

The picture emerges of a community that has started to realize the promise of the restored Israel. Through the apostles' teaching, which must have basically handed on the teaching of Jesus, and the gift of the Spirit, they are beginning to experience life under the king descended from David, "the stump of Jesse" (Isa. 11:1) on whom

> the Spirit of the LORD shall rest . . .
>> the Spirit of wisdom and understanding,
>> the Spirit of counsel and might,
>> the Spirit of knowledge and the fear of the LORD. (11:2)

The society over whom this king presides will be just, particularly with respect to the poor, who so rarely receive justice. It will also be a place of peace and abundance, like the peaceful and verdant world of the garden of Eden (11:3–9). Just as "in that day" Israel will "with joy . . . draw water from the wells of salvation" (12:1, 3) and will "sing for joy" (12:6), so these early Israelite followers of Christ Jesus are also joyful.

The early church is also a community that is beginning to see the first hints of the physical restoration of the human condition to the period before the pain, burdensome toil, and death of God's curse after Adam's disobedience (Gen. 3:17–19). The "many wonders and signs" (Acts 2:43) that the early Christian community experiences seem to have been primarily miracles of healing. Immediately after his summary of the early community's characteristics, Luke recounts the healing at the Jerusalem temple of "a man lame from birth" (3:2). "Leaping up," Luke says, "he stood and began to walk, and entered the temple with them, walking and leaping and praising God" (3:8). Isaiah had said that in the period of Israel's restoration, "the lame man" would "leap like a deer" (Isa. 35:6), and just as this had started to happen during the time of

Jesus's ministry (e.g., Matt. 9:1–8), it continues to happen among the earliest Christians. In the address that Peter gives to the crowd who assembles when the lame man is healed, Peter emphasizes this element of the new situation. He explains that faith in Jesus has given the formerly lame man "perfect health," using a term emphasizing that the man has now been restored to "wholeness" or "completeness" (Acts 3:16).[5]

The Incompleteness of the Present Restoration

Peter also makes it clear, however, that the time of Israel's, and creation's, restoration has not fully arrived. He urges the assembled crowd to turn away from their sins "that times of refreshing *may come* from the presence of the Lord, and that he *may send the Christ* appointed for you, Jesus, whom heaven must receive *until the time for restoring all things* about which God spoke by the mouth of his holy prophets long ago" (Acts 3:20–21). Peter's speech assumes that "the Author of life," as he calls Jesus, has already come, and has already been crucified and raised from the dead (3:15), but he also assumes that Jesus will come again and that, at that point, refreshing times and the restoration of all that exists will occur. Followers of Jesus live between these two great events, and so they continue to experience the hardships of life within a world that is in rebellion against its Creator at the same time that they bear witness to the inbreaking of God's new creation.

So it is not surprising that immediately after Peter's speech, the earliest Christians begin to experience great hardship and difficulty in their effort to be faithful to their new commitment to follow Christ. A particularly powerful political and religious

---

5. Henry George Liddell, Robert Scott, and Henry Stuart Jones, eds., *A Greek-English Lexicon*, rev. ed. (Oxford: Clarendon, 1996), 1217; Walter Bauer, William F. Arndt, F. Wilbur Gingrich, and F. W. Danker, eds., *A Greek-English Lexicon of the New Testament and Other Early Christian Literature*, 3rd ed. (Chicago: University of Chicago Press, 2000), 703.

group called the Sadducees, who unlike many other Jewish people do not believe in a general resurrection of the dead, have Peter and John arrested because they are teaching that the general resurrection of the dead has begun with the resurrection of Jesus from the dead (4:1–3). Not all the problems, moreover, come from outside the believing community. One couple within the group wants to appear to be participating in its communitarian approach to wealth but actually keeps back some of their property for themselves (5:1–11). God strikes them dead (5:5–6, 10), an act that must have seemed to bring the final day of God's judgment into the present.

The old and the new mix together in Luke's account. On one level, the world goes on as it always has. Roman governors, magistrates, soldiers, and local power brokers in the areas they govern are still in charge. These rulers often listen to bad advice (13:6–8), pervert justice to win favors (12:2–3), and take bribes (24:26–27). Religious hucksters still twist the truth to make themselves rich (8:9–23; cf. 13:6–8; 19:11–16), people still get sick or have accidents and die (9:36–37; 20:9), and people still exercise power over others through ethnic and religious bigotry (14:19; 16:20–21). On another level, where the apostles go, the reign of God that Jesus began to establish also goes. God's judgment sometimes falls on the wicked (12:20–23), and sometimes crippled people walk again (14:8–10), wealth is evenly distributed (20:33–35), and death itself is defeated (9:40; 20:10–12). The day of righteousness, refreshment, and restoration is drawing close but has not fully dawned.

The Nations Come to Zion

Early in Luke's account of the beginnings of this new day, he hints that it will include more than just the people of Israel. In the first few paragraphs, Jesus tells the eleven apostles that they will be his witnesses not only in Jerusalem, Judea, and Samaria, all lands traditionally within Israel's boundaries, but "to the end of the earth" (Acts 1:8). In Peter's Pentecost sermon, he makes the point that the restoration of Israel, as the prophets envisioned it, was intended eventually to include non-Israelites. "The promise," he says, "is for you and for your children and for all who are far off, everyone whom the Lord our God calls to himself" (2:39). A little later, he reminds the crowd that gathers after God has healed the lame man at the temple, "You are the sons of the prophets and of the covenant that God made with your fathers, saying to Abraham, 'And in your offspring shall all the families of the earth be blessed'" (3:25). Peter then tells these "men of Israel" (3:12) that God sent Jesus to them "first," presumably before reaching out to "all the families of the earth," and he appeals to them to repent of their wickedness and join the new movement (3:25–26). The implication is clear that God's promise to Abraham in Genesis 12:3 to bless "all the families of the earth" in him will shortly begin to be fulfilled (cf. 22:18; 26:4).

As Luke's story progresses, he shows how this promise begins to receive fulfillment in a special way through a figure named Paul. Paul is not one of the twelve apostles and not even someone who followed Jesus during his earthly ministry. Rather, he had been an enemy of the new movement until the risen Jesus powerfully intervened in his life and gave him a special commission to take to the nations the good news of God's forgiveness and desire to be at peace with his human creatures (Acts 9:1–19; 22:3–21; 26:4–23). In Acts 13:1–28:31, Luke tells the story of Paul's faithfulness to this commission as he takes the good news to both Jews and non-Jews across the eastern Mediterranean region. In a formal legal hearing before the Roman governor of Judea, Porcius Festus, and the Jewish king, Herod Agrippa II, Paul summarizes his message this way:

I stand here testifying both to small and great, saying nothing
but what the prophets and Moses said would come to pass:
that the Christ must suffer and that, by being the first to rise
from the dead, he would proclaim light both to our people
and to the Gentiles. (Acts 26:22–23)

Luke never mentions that Paul wrote letters, but thirteen of his
letters to churches and coworkers are preserved in the New Testament. He wrote them primarily to churches he had planted around
the Mediterranean or, in the case of his letters to Jesus's followers in
Rome and Colossae, to churches he had not planted but for which
he felt some responsibility. All these letters allowed Paul to teach
Jesus's followers in a wide geographical area, most of them non-Jews,
how to live in light of their new status as the restored people of God.
In two letters, he uses the phrase "new creation" to describe God's
transforming work in the lives of all who follow Jesus, whether or
not they are Jewish.

God's New Creation in Galatia

Because Paul's letter to the Galatian Christians is written to correct the teaching of a group of people who have misunderstood the
good news about Jesus (the "gospel") at what Paul considers its most
crucial point, this letter offers an energetic explanation of the gospel's most important elements. The false gospel that Paul opposes in
Galatians claims that for non-Jews to belong to the newly restored
people of God, they must not only trust that God has offered them
forgiveness and a new way of life through the death of Jesus on the
cross and the power of the Holy Spirit, but they must first become
Jews. This means accepting circumcision, a ritual commanded in
the Mosaic law (Gal. 5:2–3; 6:12–13; cf. Gen. 17:1–14; Ex. 12:48;
Lev. 12:2–3).

From the perspective of non-Jews in the Roman world, circumcision (along with Sabbath and dietary observances) is a ritual particularly distinctive of Judaism. It is what makes Jews look like Jews. In the mid-second century BC, about two hundred years before Paul wrote to the Galatians, a Syrian king named Antiochus IV Epiphanes was in control of Judea. For reasons that are not entirely clear, he prohibited the Judeans from circumcising their children and tried to force them to accept the Greek way of life, including the worship of Greek gods.[6] Many loyal Jews died rather than comply with these coercive tactics.[7] By the time of Jesus and Paul, then, a staunch commitment to the necessity of circumcision (along with Sabbath keeping and dietary observances) has become a test of real Judaism.

Like Jesus and the other apostles, however, Paul teaches that what matters is God's transformation of the human heart, and this is something that God can do within both Jews and non-Jews. Jewish Christians are certainly free to continue their ethnically distinctive observances as acts of devotion to God, but to demand these rituals of non-Jewish followers of Jesus is to badly misunderstand the law itself, the prophetic promises, and the gospel. To make distinctively Jewish elements of the Mosaic law requirements for entering the newly restored people of God is to imply that the gospel is not about God's forgiveness of the sinner through the death of Christ and the transformation of the human heart through the power of the Holy Spirit but about human effort to conform to certain entry requirements. It is to take the emphasis of the gospel off God and his gracious gifts and to place it on people and their ability to conform to certain rules. This,

---

6. See 1 Macc. 1:10–15, 41–49. For an informed discussion of Antiochus's motives, see Peter Green, *Alexander to Actium: The Historical Evolution of the Hellenistic Age*, Hellenistic Culture and Society 1 (Berkeley: University of California Press, 1990), 505–10.

7. See 1 Macc. 1:50–64.

Paul said, is "a different gospel—not that there is another one" (Gal. 1:6–7).

Paul explains the difference between the true and the false gospel by approaching it from two angles.[8] First, he explains it from the angle of the human condition. Human rebellion against God, he says, is both universal and indelible. It affects both Jews and non-Jews, and it affects them to the core of their being:

> We ourselves are Jews by birth and not Gentile sinners; yet we know that a person is not justified by works of the law but through faith in Jesus Christ, so we also have believed in Christ Jesus, in order to be justified by faith in Christ and not by works of the law, because by works of the law no one will be justified. (Gal. 2:15–16)

Paul is speaking to other Jewish people here and is saying that although non-Jewish people ("Gentiles") are commonly thought to be more sinful than Jews, what matters is not the level of sin that characterizes either group but that neither group has kept God's will as it is recorded in his law. Jews and Gentiles are united in their failure to do what God requires.

The last phrase in Paul's sentence ("because by works of the law no one will be justified") is a paraphrase of Psalm 143:2:

> Enter not into judgment with your servant,
>> for no one living is righteous before you.

Paul is speaking to people who know the Psalms well, and so he subtly makes the point that the perspective he is taking is nothing new. The Scriptures that all Jews should accept as God's word witness to

---

8. For further discussion of these two dimensions of Paul's argument, see Frank Thielman, *The Theology of the New Testament: A Canonical and Synthetic Approach* (Grand Rapids, MI: Zondervan, 2005), 266–70.

the inability of any human—Jewish or non-Jewish—to stand before God and claim that he or she is "righteous" in the most thorough sense of that term.[9]

A couple of sentences later, Paul speaks autobiographically to describe how God *does* welcome a person into his newly restored people, whether that person is Jewish or non-Jewish:

> Through the law I died to the law, so that I might live to God.
> I have been crucified with Christ. It is no longer I who live,
> but Christ who lives in me. And the life I now live in the flesh
> I live by faith in the Son of God, who loved me and gave him-
> self for me. (Gal. 2:19–20)

Paul had explained earlier in his letter that he had once been so zealous to defend the Jewish way of life as he mistakenly understood it that he had tried to stamp out the new movement of Jesus followers (1:13–14; cf. Phil. 3:6). In the midst of those efforts, God had revealed Jesus to him and transformed him from an opponent of the gospel into a proclaimer of it (Gal. 1:15–16; cf. Phil. 3:7).

Here in Galatians 2:20, he speaks of that transformation as being "crucified with Christ." Death by crucifixion was not simply another way of dying in Paul's world but a particularly shameful way of dying.[10] The crucified person's dying body hung in public, unclothed, and in great pain intentionally inflicted by the rulers of the society, supposedly because that person had committed a serious crime against society's norms. To be crucified was to experience society's best effort at making one an outcast. When Paul says that he has been "crucified with Christ," therefore, he is saying that his worldview has

---

9. For further discussion of Paul's use of Ps. 143 here and in Rom. 3:20, see especially James P. Ware, *Paul's Theology in Context: Creation, Incarnation, Covenant, and Kingdom* (Grand Rapids, MI: Eerdmans, 2019), 104–10.

10. Martin Hengel, *Crucifixion in the Ancient World and the Folly of the Message of the Cross*, trans. John Bowden (Philadelphia: Fortress, 1977).

radically changed. He has been cast out of the wider world's way of looking at life and thrust into the way of life practiced by God's newly restored people. He now lives by faith in Jesus, who showed Paul how much he loved him by dying for him.

Paul's main point is that this transformation is something God accomplishes in a person, not something a person accomplishes through adopting certain religious practices. God works this radical transformation, moreover, in all kinds of people regardless of their ethnicity, their social standing, or their gender: "There is neither Jew nor Greek, there is neither slave nor free, there is no male and female, for you are all one in Christ Jesus" (3:28). The group of individuals whom God's Spirit has transformed makes up a new society in which old, often harmful boundaries disappear or are refashioned according to God's design.[11]

Paul's second angle of approach to the difference between the false and the true gospel is historical in orientation. He reminds the Galatian Christians that God had counted Abraham's relationship with him to be right not because of Abraham's obedience to the Mosaic law but because Abraham trusted him (Gal. 3:6; cf. Gen. 15:6). This precedent, Paul argues, indicates that Gentiles who trust God to set them right with him through the death of Christ on their behalf are also right with God. Just as Abraham's faith put him right with God, so the faith of anyone in Christ, whether Jew or Gentile, puts them in a right relationship with God (Gal. 3:7). Since anyone can trust God, membership in God's newly restored people is open to both Jews and non-Jews. This arrangement, as it turns out, fulfills the promise God made to Abraham, "In you shall all the nations be blessed" (3:8–9; Gen. 12:3). The law came centuries later, and for different purposes, Paul argues, so it cannot be interpreted in a way

---

11. On the elements of both personal and societal transformation in Galatians, see Douglas J. Moo, "Creation and New Creation," *Bulletin for Biblical Research* 20, no. 1 (2010): 48–49.

that nullifies God's promise to bless the nations through Abraham (Gal. 3:15–18).

What was God's purpose in giving the law? The law, Paul says, "imprisoned everything under sin, so that the promise by faith in Jesus Christ might be given to those who believe" (3:22). God intended the law to be not the means by which people attain a right relationship with him but the means by which people understand how desperately they need God's forgiveness through Jesus Christ in order to live at peace with him. It was into the context of Israel's failure to keep the Mosaic law that Jesus came in "the fullness of time, . . . born of woman, born under the law, to redeem those who were under the law" (4:4).

Although Paul does not say so explicitly here, it is reasonably clear that he would have considered the coming of Christ to Israel to be the fulfillment of Moses's claim that one day, after Israel had experienced the curses that the law justly pronounced on God's people for their disobedience (Deut. 28:15–68), God would rescue his people from their rebellion:

> And the LORD your God will circumcise your heart and the heart of your offspring, so that you will love the LORD your God with all your heart and with all your soul, that you may live. (30:6; cf. 10:16)

The false gospel in Galatia emphasized the necessity of literal circumcision as an entry rite to the restored people of God. Paul's letter implies, however, that this "gospel" both misunderstands the human condition and misunderstands the nature of the times in which the Galatians live. Humanity is so prone to rebel against God that the only solution to this tendency is a transformed, or, as Deuteronomy might put it, a "circumcised," heart. God's people are living at the turn of the ages when the prophecy of a circumcised heart and a people restored to fellowship with himself—a people that includes all the nations of the earth—is being fulfilled.

The common element that lies beneath both of Paul's approaches to the difference between the true and the false gospel is the element of radical change. God has started to effect both a radical change within the human beings that follow Jesus and a radical change in the course of the universe. Both kinds of change converge in "the church of God" (Gal. 1:13)—the group of those who believe that God has forgiven their sins through the death of Christ and who have started to experience the transforming work of the Holy Spirit. They live under the reign of God that Jesus announced in his own preaching (5:21). This is a realm in which "sexual immorality, impurity, sensuality, idolatry, sorcery, enmity, strife, jealousy, fits of anger, rivalries, dissensions, divisions, envy, drunkenness, orgies, and things like these" are entirely out of place (5:19–21). Instead, this community values "love, joy, peace, patience, kindness, goodness, faithfulness, gentleness, self-control" (5:22–23).

This sounds like a group of people that is beginning to break free from a world where "every intention of the thoughts of [man's] heart [is] only evil continually" (Gen. 6:5) and where "sin . . . with a point of diamond . . . is engraved on the tablet of their heart" (Jer. 17:1). Paul puts it like this: "Those who belong to Christ Jesus have crucified the flesh with its passions and desires" (Gal. 5:24). Just as the Romans cast people out of their society in the firmest way through crucifixion, so those who follow Jesus have been cast out of a world in rebellion against God and into the world as God created it to be. "The world," Paul says, "has been crucified to me, and I to the world. For neither circumcision counts for anything, nor uncircumcision, but a new creation" (Gal. 6:14–15).[12]

---

12. Paul makes a similar statement a few paragraphs earlier, "For in Christ Jesus neither circumcision nor uncircumcision counts for anything, but only faith working through love"

God's New Creation in Corinth

Paul also describes followers of Jesus as part of a "new creation" in one of several letters that he writes to Christians in Corinth, a large, cosmopolitan city where Paul and his coworkers have established a church over the course of eighteen months (Acts 18:1–11). After Paul and his coworkers leave Corinth, a group of pseudoapostles arrives there (2 Cor. 11:12–15), questioning Paul's own standing as an apostle because he lacks a powerful personal presence and is not an eloquent speaker (10:1, 10; 11:6). In a letter correcting their perspective, Paul anticipates that they will also criticize him for failing to carry letters of recommendation to the various cities where he travels and proclaims the gospel (3:1).[13] Such letters were a common means of establishing social connections when traveling around the Roman world, especially for the purpose of obtaining hospitality.[14]

Paul tells the Corinthians, however, that his relationship with them does not depend on literal letters like this because he has living letters to commend the authenticity of his work as a proclaimer of the gospel:

> You yourselves are our letter of recommendation, written on our hearts to be known and read by all. And you show that you are a letter from Christ delivered by us, written not with ink but with the Spirit of the living God, not on tablets of stone but on tablets of human hearts. (2 Cor. 3:2–3)

People in the Roman world wrote not with ink on stone but with ink on papyrus, the predecessor to modern "paper." Paul is mixing his metaphors here because he wants the Corinthians to begin to think

---

(Gal. 5:6). The parallel between the "new creation" and "faith working through love" in these two statements demonstrates the quality of life that Paul believed should characterize newly created individuals. They should be people whose faith in Jesus bears the fruit of love for others.

13. Murray J. Harris, *The Second Epistle to the Corinthians: A Commentary on the Greek Text*, New International Greek Testament Commentary (Grand Rapids, MI: Eerdmans, 2005), 258–61.

14. Harris, *Second Epistle to the Corinthians*, 260.

of the stone tablets on which the finger of God wrote the Ten Words, or Ten Commandments, which summarized the covenant he had made with his people through Moses (Ex. 31:18; 32:15–16).[15]

Paul then goes on to say that God has made him and his coworkers "ministers of a new covenant, not of the letter but of the Spirit. For the letter kills, but the Spirit gives life" (2 Cor. 3:6). The word "letter" here refers not to a letter of recommendation but to a letter of the alphabet (the two terms are actually different words in Paul's Greek). Paul is thinking of how God engraved the Mosaic covenant on stone tablets, writing in letters of the Hebrew alphabet. When he uses the term "new covenant," Paul is referencing the only place in the Hebrew Scriptures where the term "new covenant" appears, Jeremiah 31:31–34:

> Behold, the days are coming, declares the Lord, when I will make a *new covenant* with the house of Israel and the house of Judah, not like the covenant that I made with their fathers on the day when I took them by the hand to bring them out of the land of Egypt, my covenant that they broke, though I was their husband, declares the Lord. For this is the covenant that I will make with the house of Israel after those days, declares the Lord: I will *put my law within them*, and I will *write it on their hearts*. And I will be their God, and they shall be my people. And no longer shall each one teach his neighbor and each his brother, saying, "Know the Lord," for they shall all know me, from the least of them to the greatest, declares the Lord. For I will forgive their iniquity, and I will remember their sin no more.

Paul's defense of his failure to carry literal letters of recommendation implies that he and the Corinthian Christians are living in the

---

15. See Frank Thielman, *Paul and the Law: A Contextual Approach* (Downers Grove, IL: InterVarsity Press, 1994), 109–10.

time when Jeremiah's prophecy of a new covenant is being fulfilled. "The letter kills" (2 Cor. 3:6) not because there is anything wrong with the Mosaic law. Rather, as Jeremiah 31:31–34 implies, the fault lies with the hearts of the people who break the law. The law justly pronounces the sentence of death on the rebellion of God's people against him.[16]

Now, however, the Spirit of God has transformed the hearts of Paul and the Corinthian Christians so that they are beginning to live in the way God designed human beings to live. The Holy Spirit has written God's law "within them," on their hearts. To use the language of Deuteronomy, God has circumcised their hearts (Deut. 30:6; cf. 10:16), or to use the language of Ezekiel, God has given them a new heart and put a new Spirit within them (Ezek. 36:26). Paul cannot imagine a better "letter of recommendation" for his proclamation of the gospel than that real, visible transformation in the lives of people who have heard and accepted his message.

A few sentences later (2 Cor. 3:18), Paul explains that those who are part of this new covenant community have, in a sense, seen the glory of God himself. In this way they are like Moses, who in his own time was the only person who saw God, in contrast to the rest of Israel (Ex. 33:23; Num. 12:8).[17] Paul is probably thinking of the way God's character is clearly portrayed in Jesus, as Jesus is described in the gospel. A little later in his argument, Paul characterizes those who reject the gospel as failing to see "the light of the gospel of the glory of Christ, who is the image of God" (2 Cor. 4:4).[18] This vision

---

16. For more on this theme, see Thielman, *Paul and the Law*, 110–12.

17. Harris, *Second Epistle to the Corinthians*, 313.

18. Paul may also be alluding to Isa. 9:2 here:

The people who walked in darkness
    have seen a great light;
those who dwelt in a land of deep darkness,
    on them has light shone.

On this possibility, see Moyer V. Hubbard, *New Creation in Paul's Letters and Thought*, Society for New Testament Studies Monograph Series 119 (Cambridge: Cambridge University Press,

of God in Jesus, Paul says, is transformative for those who experience it. They are "being transformed into the same image from one degree of glory to another" (3:18). Paul seems to be saying that as believers yield themselves more and more to the vision of God as he appears in the Jesus of the gospel, they increasingly reflect the image of God that they see.[19] This mention of human beings reflecting the "image" of God recalls the creation of man and woman in God's "image" and "likeness" according to Genesis 1:26–27 (cf. 5:1; 9:6). Those who follow Jesus become increasingly like Jesus, and as they become more like Jesus, they become both more human and more like God himself.

All this, Paul says, is similar to God's creative action at the beginning of the world. "God, who said, 'Let light shine out of darkness,' has shone in our hearts to give the light of the knowledge of the glory of God in the face of Jesus Christ" (2 Cor. 4:6). A few paragraphs later, Paul describes the effect of the reconciliation between God and human beings that he proclaims this way:

> From now on, therefore, we regard no one according to the flesh. Even though we once regarded Christ according to the flesh, we regard him thus no longer. Therefore, if anyone is in Christ, he is a new creation. The old has passed away; behold, the new has come. (5:16–17)

Paul speaks here of the transformation that takes place in the outlook of anyone who is "in Christ," that is, anyone who trusts and follows him.[20] The person whom God has transformed looks at people in a way that differs from the world around him or her (5:16a). The way Paul's own understanding of Christ was transformed provides

---

2002), 160. If this is correct, then Paul may also be hinting that those who reject Christ are rejecting the Messiah of prophetic expectation.

19. Harris, *Second Epistle to the Corinthians*, 316–17.

20. Cf. Hubbard, *New Creation*, 179–83.

an example of this perspective (5:16b). Before he became a Christian, he agreed with the powerful and influential politicians in charge of Judea about Christ. He thought of Christ and his followers as troublemakers that needed to be eliminated (Acts 7:58; 8:1–3; 22:4–5; 26:9–12), but then God stood Paul's view of Christ on its head (Acts 9:1–19; 22:6–21; 26:13–23). As the stunned churches of Judea said at the time, "He who used to persecute us is now preaching the faith he once tried to destroy" (Gal. 1:23; cf. Acts 9:21, 26).

Paul had himself been re-created, and he had joined a community that was becoming part of the new creation. This was a group of people who had been reconciled to God through the death of Christ on their behalf and who were now ambassadors of this new society (2 Cor. 5:18–21). They were proclaiming to others that the new exodus of Isaiah 43:18–19 was under way:

> Remember not the former things,
>   nor consider the things of old.
> Behold, I am doing a new thing;
>   now it springs forth, do you not perceive it?

They were calling people to recognize that Isaiah 49:8 had been fulfilled:

> In a favorable time I listened to you,
>   and in a day of salvation I have helped you. (2 Cor. 6:2)[21]

The gospel was an invitation to everyone to be reconciled to God and to join this community of newly created humanity, just as Paul himself had done.

---

21. On Paul's use of Isaiah's new-creation motif in 2 Cor. 5:1–6:2, see T. Ryan Jackson, *New Creation in Paul's Letters: A Study of the Historical and Social Setting of a Pauline Concept*, Wissenschaftliche Untersuchungen zum Neuen Testament, 2nd ser., vol. 272 (Tübingen: Mohr Siebeck, 2010), 116–27, 179. See also Moo, "Creation and New Creation," 54.

Paul makes it clear in this letter to Corinth, just as he had made it clear in his letter to the Galatian Christians, that God's work of new creation in the individual produces more than a mental transformation. This reorientation of one's worldview yields practical results. The gospel teaches that God has graciously reconciled himself to his human creatures through Christ. Those who have received this gift from God, Paul says, should also live in peace with others.[22] So he appeals to the Corinthians to be reconciled to him:

> We have spoken freely to you, Corinthians; our heart is wide open. You are not restricted by us, but you are restricted in your own affections. In return (I speak as to children) widen your hearts also. (2 Cor. 6:11–13)

Paul also asks them to give generously to a collection that he is taking up for needy fellow believers in Jerusalem (9:12; cf. Rom. 15:26; 1 Cor. 16:1–4):

> For I do not mean that others should be eased and you burdened, but that as a matter of fairness your abundance at the present time should supply their need, so that their abundance may supply your need, that there may be fairness. (2 Cor. 8:13–14)

Just as Luke described how the early Christians held their property in common with the result that there were no needy people among them, so here Paul urges the Corinthian Christians to work at economic equity among all Christians. Since the Corinthian Christians are mainly non-Jewish and the Jerusalem Christians are chiefly Jewish, moreover, this offering is a demonstration of the gospel's tendency to dissolve the social barriers that stand in the way of peaceful

---

22. Harris, *Second Epistle to the Corinthians*, 487.

relationships among ethnic groups. The "new creation" is to be a place of kindness, justice, and peace.

Conclusion

With the coming of the Holy Spirit on the followers of Jesus, then, God has begun to form his restored people. As the prophets predicted, this new people would begin with a new Israel formed of Jewish people both from Judea and from the lands where they had been scattered. Quickly, however, it begins to expand to non-Jewish people, especially through a traveling team of Christ followers who work with the apostle Paul. Essentially, "many peoples" are coming to a figurative Zion and saying,

> Come, let us go up to the mountain of the LORD,
>   to the house of the God of Jacob,
> that he may teach us his ways
>   and that we may walk in his paths. (Isa. 2:3)

The apostles consider this new people to be the beginning of a re-created human society in which people relate to one another in ways that model God's creation before human rebellion sends society into a downward spiral of mistrust, resentment, violence, greed, and lust for power. The "church of God" is a place that at least holds up the societal ideals of love, justice, kindness, and peace—all of it based on the character of God as shown through Jesus, the great Davidic king of prophetic expectation.

5

Living as God's New Humanity
Now and in the Future

Paul's letter to the Ephesians and John's prophecy in Revelation describe particularly clearly what new-creation life should look like in the present and what it will look like in the future. Both texts are written to Christians in large cities in the Roman province of Asia, and a large Roman city was, for most who lived there, a difficult place to carve out an existence. The following tomb inscription from Rome itself, which shows up more than once in the archaeological record, probably represents the experience of many people: "Bones reposing sweetly, I am not anxious about suddenly being short of food. I do not suffer from arthritis, and I am not indebted because of being behind in my rent. In fact my lodgings are permanent—and free!"[1] Life was hard and marked by competition for survival between individuals and the various groups to which they belonged.[2]

---

1. Nicholas Purcell, trans., "Life in the City," in *The World of Rome: An Introduction to Roman Culture*, ed. Peter Jones and Keith Sidwell (Cambridge: Cambridge University Press, 1997), 148.

2. See especially Jerry Toner, *Popular Culture in Ancient Rome* (Cambridge: Polity, 2009).

Following Jesus within the community of the new creation added a layer of complexity and difficulty to an already difficult life because Christians stood apart from the culture around them and were often marginalized by it. Ephesus, for example, was known as a center for the dark arts. People often used magical incantations and attempts to manipulate the gods in order to make life go their way or to squash their competition.[3] So when Paul's proclamation of the gospel began to take root in Ephesus, it is not surprising to find Luke recording that "a number of those who had practiced magic arts brought their books together and burned them in the sight of all" (Acts 19:19) and that worship of the goddess Artemis, whose shrine was in Ephesus, fell into disrepute among the "many people" whom Paul had persuaded (19:26–27). The result was a public riot against Christianity in Ephesus (19:28–41).

According to Richard Bauckham, the Christians to whom John writes Revelation frequently faced the dilemma of either sacrificing their social standing and participation in civic life or engaging in idolatrous rituals and immoral behaviors that were an integral part of urban life, especially for anyone who was affluent or a member of the upper classes.[4]

Both Paul and John are writing to believers out of their own experiences of suffering for their commitment to Jesus. Paul writes to the Ephesian Christians from house arrest in Rome (Eph. 3:1, 13; 4:1; 6:20; cf. Acts 28:16, 30). He writes to encourage his readers in light of the hardship they see him going through (Eph. 3:13) and are probably going through themselves.[5] His letter provides them with a

---

3. Clinton E. Arnold, *Power and Magic: The Concept of Power in Ephesians* (Grand Rapids, MI: Baker, 1992), 14–20.

4. Richard Bauckham, *The Theology of the Book of Revelation*, New Testament Theology (Cambridge: Cambridge University Press, 1993), 128.

5. On this, see Frank Thielman, *Ephesians*, Baker Exegetical Commentary on the New Testament (Grand Rapids, MI: Baker Academic, 2010), 16–19.

refresher course on how to live as part of the new creation within a world that has not yet been restored.

John writes from Patmos, a Greek island to which he has been exiled "on account of the word of God and the testimony of Jesus" (Rev. 1:9).[6] He writes to a wide variety of Christians. Some of his audience are patiently suffering for their commitment to Jesus instead of compromising their faith (2:3, 9, 13, 24; 3:4, 8, 10). Others are in grave danger of bending their commitment to Christ in unfaithful ways in order to fit into the corrupt social systems in the large cities in which they live (2:14–15, 20–23; 3:1–3, 15–19).[7]

Christ and His People as the New Humanity in Ephesians

Paul begins his letter of encouragement to the Ephesian Christians with a lengthy prayer of praise to God for all that God has done for them (Eph. 1:3–14). He then issues a report on what he thanks God for when he prays for them (1:15–16) and what he prays that God might do for them (1:17–23). His prayers on behalf of the Ephesian Christians focus on his hope that God will give them the spiritual eyes they need in order to see the great power God has used to transform them into his renewed people (1:19–2:22).

In describing that great power, Paul turns first to an analogy. God, he says, is so powerful that he was able to raise Christ from the dead and seat him in a royal place of honor, at his right hand, "in the heavenly places" (1:20). That high position corresponds to Christ's authority over all other powerful forces in the universe, "all rule and authority and power and dominion" (1:21). Paul then uses a line from

---

6. Elsewhere in Revelation when people experience something on account of "the word of God" and on account of "the testimony of Jesus" (20:4; cf. 6:9), they are experiencing persecution for their commitment to Jesus. On this pattern, see Henry Barclay Swete, *The Apocalypse of St. John*, 3rd ed. (London: Macmillan, 1911), 12–13; G. K. Beale, *The Book of Revelation: A Commentary on the Greek Text*, New International Greek Testament Commentary (Grand Rapids, MI: Eerdmans, 1999), 202.

7. Bauckham, *Revelation*, 128–29.

Psalm 8, "And he put all things under his feet" (Eph. 1:22; cf. Ps. 8:6). Within Psalm 8, this line does not refer to the military might of the great Davidic king, as we might expect (cf. Pss. 2:7–8; 110:1), but to God's gift to the first man and woman of dominion over the animal world in Genesis 1:26–28. Paul seems to be hinting that the Messiah, whom God raised from the dead and seated at his right hand, is also a new Adam (cf. 1 Cor. 15:20–28, 42–49).[8] He then makes the point that when the Ephesians decided to follow Jesus, God used his great power in a way that was analogous to the resurrection of Christ. He raised them from the spiritual death of living in rebellion against him and united them to the risen Christ (Eph. 2:1–6). In a sense, they are now "seated . . . with him in the heavenly places" (2:6).

Because of this, they, too, are re-created human beings. "For we are his workmanship," Paul asserts, "created in Christ Jesus for good works, which God prepared beforehand, that we should walk in them" (2:10). Paul's terms "workmanship" and "created" recall the picture in Genesis 2:7 of God the potter forming the first man from the clay of the ground and breathing "into his nostrils the breath of life" so that he might become "a living creature."

The continuation of Paul's argument (Eph. 2:11–22) implies that when Christians are re-created by God in this way, they are not merely remade as individuals, but they become part of a new society, which Paul can also describe, in the singular, as a "new man" (2:15).[9] They are no longer defined by the competing and often hostile social groups to which they formerly belonged. Rather, Christ refashions members of these groups when they put their trust in him "that he might create in himself one new man . . . , so making peace" (2:15).

---

8. John Eadie, *Commentary on the Epistle to the Ephesians*, 3rd ed. (Edinburgh: T&T Clark, 1883), 104; S. M. Baugh, *Ephesians*, Evangelical Exegetical Commentary (Bellingham, WA: Lexham, 2016), 128–29.

9. See the study of Ephesians by John R. W. Stott, appropriately titled *God's New Society: The Message of Ephesians* (Downers Grove, IL: InterVarsity Press, 1979).

Because everyone within this group has been reconciled to God through Christ's death on the cross (2:16), they are also reconciled to one another and live at peace with each other. They all "have access in one Spirit to the Father" (2:18).

Paul then shifts to a new, architectural metaphor to describe the unity Christians have with one another across various social boundaries. It is as if they are all parts of a single building (2:20–22). The foundation of the building is formed by the Christian apostles and prophets who brought the Ephesians the gospel (2:20a). Christ Jesus himself is the most important stone in the building (2:20b), and everything is dependent on him for support (2:21). The Ephesian Christians, together with all other Christians, are also part of the structure of this building, attached as they are to Christ and to one another, and the building itself is "a dwelling place for God by the Spirit" (2:22).

The building, then, is actually a temple. Just as the biblical tabernacle and temple in Jerusalem were places where God revealed his presence with his people, so now, Paul says, God is present with all his people all the time. The picture emerges in 2:11–22 of a society full of peace and the presence of God. In these ways, it resembles the garden of Eden or the vision of blessing in Leviticus 26:3–13, in which, as God says,

> I will give peace in the land, and you shall lie down, and none shall make you afraid. . . . I will make my dwelling among you, and my soul shall not abhor you. And I will walk among you and will be your God, and you shall be my people. (Lev. 26:6, 11–12)

Paul hopes that this picture of all that God has done for the Ephesian Christians in Christ will encourage them not to give up on their trust in God in the midst of the hardship that both he and they are experiencing.

Paul's Advice on How God's New Humanity Should Live

Paul also wants to provide practical guidance to the Ephesian Christians for how they should live as God's new creatures, especially how they should live in harmony with one another. They should, he says, live with each other in humility, gentleness, patience, love, unity, and peace (Eph. 4:1–3).

Their unity with each other should reflect the unity of God himself (4:4–6). Although God exists in a diversity of persons—Father, Son, and Holy Spirit—he is, nevertheless, one being. In the same way, those who follow Christ have a diversity of gifts and roles in their new society, but each person should use his or her abilities to help the entire body of Christians attain a full and unified understanding of who Christ is and the meaning of faith in him (4:4–13).

As he develops this theme, Paul describes those who are committed to following Christ as "the body of Christ" (4:12). He then describes this body as growing "to mature manhood, to the measure of the stature of the fullness of Christ" (4:13). The phrase "to mature manhood" is probably more than just a general reference to the process by which a boy becomes a man. Its gender specificity may be a way of urging the letter's audience to think of the first man, Adam. If so, then the next phrase ("to the measure of the stature of the fullness of Christ") would portray Christ as a new Adam. As the "body of Christ," Paul seems to be saying that the church is growing into the kind of human being that Christ was and still is, and Christ is the sort of human being that God created all people to be.

Growth in treating other people with humility, gentleness, patience, and love, and growth in understanding who Christ is and what trust in him entails, therefore, is growth in becoming what God designed human beings to be when he created them. Christ is the "perfect man," and Christians are a society of people on their way to becoming what he is in this sense.

A few sentences later, Paul contrasts the way of life that his audience practiced before they trusted in Christ with the way of life that should now characterize them. People in Ephesus who do not follow Christ, he says, "have given themselves over to sensuality so as to indulge in every kind of impurity, and they are full of greed" (Eph. 4:19 NIV). Those who trust Christ, however, have learned to "lay aside the old man who is being corrupted in accordance with deceitful desires, to be renewed in the spirit of [their] mind, and to put on the new man who has been created in God's image—in righteousness and holiness that comes from truth" (4:22–24 NET). As the phrase "created in God's image" shows, the references to "the old man" and "the new man" echo both the Genesis story of human rebellion against God and the prophetic hints that God would eventually make the human heart capable of doing his will, as it was when God created it. Since Christians are the beginning of the new humanity, Paul is saying, they should be characterized not by sexual immorality and greed but by righteousness and holiness, as those qualities are defined by the truth of God's word.[10]

Paul then gives a list of behaviors (4:25–5:2) that provide examples of what he means by "righteousness and holiness that comes from truth" (4:24 NET). Christians who are truly living in the way God created human beings to live, Paul says, will speak truthfully, control their anger, stop stealing, and work hard so that they can give to the needy. They will avoid unedifying speech and instead build others up with gracious words. They will cooperate with God's desire to remove from them all hurtful and angry words and, out of

---

10. On this understanding of the phrase "righteousness and holiness that comes from truth" (Eph. 4:24 NET), see Thielman, *Ephesians*, 307.

hearts of compassion, will forgive those who do them wrong. Paul summarizes this list by returning to the idea of God's re-creation of humanity so that it might reflect his image more perfectly:

> Therefore be imitators of God, as beloved children. And walk in love, as Christ loved us and gave himself up for us, a fragrant offering and sacrifice to God. (5:1–2)

As people created in God's image, human beings reflect that image best when they imitate in their behavior toward others the love God has shown to them. That love was shown clearly in the sacrificial death of Christ that restored a peaceful relationship between God and human beings.

A few paragraphs later, Paul illustrates how this kind of sacrificial love works itself out in the Christian family, and he begins with the relationship between husband and wife. His instructions focus primarily on husbands, who, he says, should imitate Christ's love for the church in their love for their wives. Christ "gave himself up for" the church's well-being, and so "in the same way husbands should love their wives as their own bodies" (5:25, 28). Paul then quotes from Genesis 2:24, "Therefore a man shall leave his father and mother and hold fast to his wife, and the two shall become one flesh" (Eph. 5:31). "This mystery is profound," he continues, "and I am saying that it refers to Christ and the church" (5:32). When husband and wife live in loving unity with each other, then, they fulfill one of God's main purposes in instituting marriage at the time of the world's creation. Marriage was intended to illustrate the love of Christ for his people.

Paul concludes his letter with a rousing call to arms that sends his readers forth dressed in "the whole armor of God" (6:11; cf. 6:10–18).[11] His piece-by-piece description of this "armor" echoes the simi-

---

11. Cf. Andrew T. Lincoln, *Ephesians*, Word Biblical Commentary 42 (Dallas: Word Books, 1990), 433–34.

lar use of this metaphor in Isaiah 59. There, however, God is wearing the armor precisely because he cannot find anyone else willing to wear it. Isaiah tells of the Lord's dismay at the injustice and falsehood that characterized Israelite society at that time:

> The LORD saw it, and it displeased him
> that there was no justice. (Isa. 59:15)

And he saw further that there was no person willing to intercede and bring justice and truth to society (59:16). So the Lord himself brought justice and truth:

> He put on righteousness as a breastplate,
> and a helmet of salvation on his head. (59:17)

He then rushed headlong into the battle against injustice and falsehood and brought with him both judgment for the wicked and redemption for anyone willing to repent (59:17–20).

For Paul, the new people of God also move forward into a world full of rebellion against God, with all its injustice and oppression, and do so dressed in "the armor of God" (Eph. 6:11) to defend themselves against the onslaught of evil as they work for truth and righteousness (6:14). They carry out their work dressed in the peace that the gospel brings, in their trust in God, in the salvation they have received, and in their devotion to the word of God and prayer (6:15–18). There is no hint here that Christians should effect God's judgment on society, as the armor-clad God of Isaiah 59:17–18 does. That task is for God alone (Rom. 12:19). Before the final day of judgment and redemption, however, God's people can and should be the people God looks for in Isaiah 59:16. As the people of God who wear the armor of God, they should work for justice and truth within the church and in the societies in which they live.

John's Vision of the New Creation as a City, a Bride, and a Temple

John, the author of Revelation, also urges the church to live as God's people within a world in rebellion against God, and specifically within the world of the mid-first-century Roman Empire. As part of his encouragement to his readers to remain faithful, however, John points beyond the present to the new creation of the future and vividly describes the world of peace in the presence of God that those who follow Jesus will one day inhabit. His description brings the story of creation full circle, back to the human experience of the palpable presence of God that characterized the existence of humanity in the garden according to Genesis 2–3.

John describes this vision in Revelation 21:1–22:5, at the end of his prophetic call to God's people not to compromise with Rome's injustice, oppression, and idolatry. Just before that passage, he describes Rome and her dominion over the Mediterranean world imaginatively as "the great prostitute who is seated on many waters," and he envisions the social groups who have aligned themselves with Rome's oppressive tactics to their own economic benefit as "the kings of the earth" who "have committed sexual immorality" with her (17:1–2). The church, John says, must stand apart from all this and resist compromise with Rome's idolatry and injustice:

> Come out of her, my people,
>   lest you take part in her sins,
> lest you share in her plagues;
> for her sins are heaped high as heaven,
>   and God has remembered her iniquities. (18:4–5)

John knows that the church's refusal to go along with normal Roman society will plunge it into suffering, and throughout his book he has referred to those willing to endure hardship in order to remain faithful to Jesus paradoxically as those who "conquer" (2:7, 11, 17, 26; 3:5, 12).[12] God has given them victory over evil in the same way that he gave Jesus victory over evil—through the pathway of suffering (3:21; 12:11). Just as Jesus, the sacrificial Lamb of God, was slaughtered in order to ransom a people for God "from every tribe and language and people and nation" (5:9; cf. Isa. 53:7; Rev. 7:9), so this newly formed people of God "follow[s] the Lamb wherever he goes," including to death if necessary (14:4), and "they have washed their robes and made them white in the blood of the Lamb" (7:14).[13] They form a multinational, multiethnic group of people who have faithfully followed Jesus by not compromising with the world around them in its rebellion against God.

One day, John envisions, God will judge and punish societies like Rome's. He will also justly judge the pseudo-Christians who have compromised with the idolatry, injustice, and deceit of such societies for their own gain (18:1–20:15). John's description of the new creation follows his picture of that judgment. In the "new heaven" and "new earth," God will give the blessing of his presence to all those who have faithfully followed the Lamb despite the hardship this has entailed (21:1–8; cf. Isa. 65:17; 66:22).

John's description of this new universe recalls the accounts of creation and of life in the garden in Genesis 1–3, where God spoke directly with the first man and woman (2:16–17; 3:9–19), walked among them (3:8), and provided for their every need (2:9, 16, 18–25; 3:21).[14] The most important blessing of the church's new existence will be its similar experience of the immediate, palpable presence of God. John communicates this reality by describing the new creation

---

12. For what follows in this paragraph, see Bauckham, *Revelation*, 69–80.
13. Bauckham, *Revelation*, 77.
14. Bauckham, *Revelation*, 140.

in a kaleidoscope of three images: a city, a bride, and God's "dwelling," the temple:

> Then I saw a new heaven and a new earth; for the first heaven and the first earth had passed away, and the sea was no more. I also saw the holy *city*, the new Jerusalem, coming down out of heaven from God, prepared like a *bride* adorned for her husband. Then I heard a loud voice from the throne: Look, God's *dwelling* is with humanity, and he will live with them. They will be his peoples, and God himself will be with them and will be their God. (Rev. 21:1–3 CSB)

First, John describes the life of God's people in the new creation as life in a city. It is "the holy city, the new Jerusalem, coming down out of heaven from God" (21:2 CSB). In stark contrast to the wicked city of Rome, which John has a little earlier compared to the great and evil city Babylon in Israel's Scriptures (17:5, 9; 18:2, 10, 21; cf. Isa. 13:19; 14:3–23; 21:9), this new city is holy. Like the biblical Jerusalem, moreover, it is the place of the temple, the symbol of God's presence.[15]

A few sentences later, John describes this city as "having the glory of God, its radiance like a most rare jewel, like a jasper, clear as crystal" (Rev. 21:11). This description recalls John's much earlier account of God himself, seated on his heavenly throne and having "the appearance of jasper and carnelian," surrounded by "a rainbow that had the appearance of an emerald," with a "sea of glass, like crystal" stretched out before him (4:3, 6). It also recalls the Lord's promise in Isaiah to make a "covenant of peace" with his people and to restore their fortunes so fully that he would lay the foundations of

---

15. Bauckham, *Revelation*, 126–32.

their society with "lapis lazuli" and would make "their battlements of jasper," their "gates of crystal stones," and their "enclosure of precious stones" (Isa. 54:11–12 NETS). This city, then, will be a place of God's presence and therefore a place of both beauty and peace.

John also describes the city in a way that emphasizes the number twelve. Its high wall has twelve gates, with twelve angels stationed at each gate and the names of the twelve tribes of Israel inscribed on the gates. The city has four sides with three gates each, and each side is oriented to a point of the compass. It has twelve foundations, and on them are inscribed "the twelve names of the twelve apostles of the Lamb" (Rev. 21:12–14). The number twelve symbolizes God's people through all history, and the four cardinal directions (21:13) perhaps hint that the new creation will reach across the world and include people from "every tribe and language and people and nation" (5:9; cf. 7:9; 21:24; 22:2).

All this imagery combines to communicate that the new creation will be a place in which God himself lives with his people in a beautiful, multiethnic, and peaceful environment. This environment is reminiscent of the garden in Eden, but it is also an urban environment, perhaps because the number of God's people assembled down through history is so great.

Second, John describes the experience of God's people in the new creation as a bride dressed for her wedding day (21:2, 9; cf. 19:7). At first, it may seem odd and abrupt to jump from the image of a city to the image of a bride to describe God's presence with his people. Cities, however, were often pictured as women in the cultural context in which John lived.[16] The goddess Roma, the personification of Rome, for example, could appear in artwork of the period as an elegantly dressed woman with her right arm curled around a spear

---

16. Bauckham, *Revelation*, 126.

and a sword on her left hip, seated next to the Emperor Augustus, and surrounded by symbols of an idyllic world of peace and plenty.[17] John knew that a message like this was nothing but propaganda. Rome had established its dominance in the world through violence, oppression, and injustice, and it continued to use these means to maintain a life of luxury for the few powerful and wealthy people in its empire. John's feisty counterimage proposes that "Roma" is actually "the great prostitute" (17:1), who uses her power to serve her own, selfish interests.[18]

He then contrasts her with the beautiful and pure people of God as the bride of the Lamb. The contrast becomes clear in the almost identical way that John introduces his picture of the two city-women. Rome and the new Jerusalem both come into the narrative through "one of the seven angels who had the seven bowls," and that angel introduces each city-woman in similar but contrasting terms. "Come," he says to John in Revelation 17:1, "I will show you the judgment of the great prostitute," and then in 21:9, "Come, I will show you the Bride, the wife of the Lamb" (cf. 19:7).[19] John envisions a future in which God's people constitute a new and beautiful "bride adorned for her husband" (Rev. 21:2), and her husband is Jesus himself.

Unlike Paul in Ephesians, John does not quote from or even allude to the Genesis narrative of the first marriage (Gen. 2:18–25). From a theological perspective, however, it is a short step from what John does say to the conclusion that in the new creation Christ's preparation of the church as a bride "without spot or wrinkle or any such thing" (Eph. 5:27) finds its fulfillment. If that is so, then the profound mystery of marriage that Paul describes in Ephesians 5:31

---

17. See the mid-first-century *Gemma Augustea* in Vienna's Kunsthistorische Museum. A photograph of this intricately carved cameo appears in Roger Ling, "Roman Art and Architecture," in Jones and Sidwell, *World of Rome*, 307.

18. Bauckham, *Revelation*, 126.

19. Swete, *Apocalypse of St. John*, 283.

with a quotation from Genesis 2:24 also finds its ultimate meaning in the presence of God with his people in the new heavens and the new earth.

Third, John describes the life of God's people in God's presence using the imagery of the tabernacle and temple, the structures that symbolized God's presence with Israel. In the ancient Greek edition of Exodus, an edition John knew, the term for the tabernacle from Exodus 25 forward is precisely the same term that John uses for God's future "dwelling" in the new creation:

> Then I heard a loud voice from the throne: Look, God's *dwelling* is with humanity, and he will live with them. They will be his peoples, and God himself will be with them and will be their God. (Rev. 21:3 CSB)

The Hebrew word that lies beneath this term also appears in the climactic blessing God gives to those who keep his commandments in Leviticus 26:11–12:

> I will make my *dwelling* among you, and my soul shall not abhor you. And I will walk among you and will be your God and you shall be my people.

John not only recalls this blessing in Leviticus, but he broadens it so that it applies beyond the "people" of Israel to "humanity" generally, made up of various "peoples."

The prophet Ezekiel had already described the worldwide effect of Leviticus 26:11–12 when he recalled it in connection with "the covenant of peace" that God would eventually establish with Israel through a great shepherd-king like David:

> David my servant shall be their prince forever. I will make a covenant of peace with them. It shall be an everlasting

covenant with them. And I will set them in their land and multiply them, and will set my sanctuary in their midst forevermore. My dwelling place shall be with them, and I will be their God, and they shall be my people. Then the nations will know that I am the LORD who sanctifies Israel, when my sanctuary is in their midst forevermore. (Ezek. 37:25–28)[20]

A few decades later, Zechariah looked forward to a day when God would "dwell" in the "midst" of his people and to a time when "many nations" would "join themselves to the LORD" (Zech. 2:11).

John probably alludes to all these prophecies, and behind them all stands the vision of a time before and shortly after God's first creatures rebelled against him, when God spoke with them directly, walked in their midst, and made clothing for them (Gen. 2:15–17; 3:8–21). In the garden, God's presence was so palpable that there was no need for a temple, or, to put it another way, the whole garden was a temple. In the same way, John imagines the new creation as a city that has no temple (Rev. 21:22) but is itself a temple. Its cubic shape imitates the cubic shape of the temple's most holy place, the place most symbolic of God's presence (21:15–16; cf. 1 Kings 6:20), and the jasper, emerald, carnelian, and gold that beautifully adorn its features are reminiscent not only of the appearance of God in John's vision (Rev. 4:2–3) but also of the garden in Eden, which was located in a place rich with precious minerals and metals (Gen. 2:11–12; Ezek. 28:13).[21]

As John concludes his vision of the heavenly temple-city in Revelation 22:1–5, references to the garden become more explicit. "The river of the water of life" (22:1) that flows from the throne of God

20. Beale, *Revelation*, 1046–47.
21. Bauckham, *Revelation*, 133–34.

and the Lamb is reminiscent of the river that "flowed out of Eden to water the garden" (Gen. 2:10). "The tree of life" that grows "on either side of the river" (Rev. 22:2) clearly recalls "the tree of life . . . in the midst of the garden" (Gen. 2:9). This tree, John says, will yield twelve kinds of fruit and will yield that fruit every month. Just as in the garden of Eden, God will supply all the needs of his people, and since the tree of life conferred immortality in the garden (Gen. 3:22), its presence here is a reminder that God will take care of his people forever. As John says in Revelation 21:4, God "will wipe away every tear from their eyes, and death shall be no more, neither shall there be mourning, nor crying, nor pain anymore, for the former things have passed away" (cf. Isa. 25:6–8).

The new creation, then, will be the home of the "great multitude that no one [can] number, from every nation, from all tribes and peoples and languages" (Rev. 7:9; cf. 5:9; 22:2), who have followed the Lamb through the ages since the time of Adam. Their fellowship with God will be fully restored, never to be broken again. "They will see his face" (22:4) and will live forever within the world as God created it to be.

Conclusion

The honest person looking around at the world's societies today has to admit that not much has changed since the time of Adam, Isaiah, Matthew, Paul, and John. The world is still a long way from John's vision of nations walking in peace on the earth by the light of God's glory (Rev. 21:23–24; cf. 22:2). Lamech's chest-thumping threats of domestic violence to the two women under his power in Genesis 4:23–24 sound like the story of too many women today. If justice, righteousness, and truth were people, many governments, academic institutions, and media outlets today would turn Justice away and keep Righteousness at arm's length. As in Isaiah's day, Truth can still be found stumbling around "in the public squares" (Isa. 59:14) because it cannot find adequate footing.[22] "He who departs from evil makes himself a prey" (Isa. 59:15) could be a placard over the workplace of many employees.

The greed, sexual immorality, and alienation from God that figured so prominently in Paul's description of the world in which the Ephesian Christians were immersed (Eph. 2:1–3, 11–12; 4:19; 5:3–6) also continue to describe today's world. John's picture of the Roman government violently exploiting both the earth and its people groups, including, but not limited to, Christians, sounds all too familiar (Rev. 17:1–18:24). Many people go through their daily routines and many governments form and enact their policies without giving God a passing thought. Large corporations knowingly exploit the environment and the people who work for them for their own profit. Sexual assault, racism, and nationalism regularly feature in the news. In many academic, political, and entertainment contexts, sexual promiscuity is assumed to be permissible, and "marriage" has become a controversial topic. Clearly, the world continues to labor under the effects of human rebellion against God.[23]

Because he is "merciful and gracious, slow to anger, and abounding in steadfast love and faithfulness," however, God did not leave his human creatures helpless within the world they created for themselves (Ex. 34:6; cf. Num. 14:18; Neh. 9:17; Pss. 86:15; 103:8; 145:8; Joel 2:13; Jonah 4:2). He gave them Jesus, and Jesus gave to those who trusted him the Holy Spirit, and the Holy Spirit gave Jesus's followers a new society, the church. The church, when it is

---

22. On Isaiah's use of personification in this brilliant passage, see Paul R. House, *Isaiah*, Mentor Commentary, 2 vols. (Fearn, Ross-shire, Scotland: Mentor, 2019), 2:596–97.

23. On this point, see the insightful analysis of Cornelius Plantinga Jr., *Not the Way It's Supposed to Be: A Breviary of Sin* (Grand Rapids, MI: Eerdmans, 1995).

rightly built on the foundation of the apostles and prophets, now found in the Scriptures, and with Christ as that foundation's most important stone, is what S. M. Baugh has aptly called "the embassy of the inaugurated new creation."[24] The church is a group of people in whom the Spirit of God is at work, helping them live more and more in the way that God created human beings to live: trusting God as he is revealed in Jesus Christ, working at the tasks he has given them to do without greed, and advancing human society through loving families.

When the Christians who make up the church pursue these tasks with the same love, kindness, and generosity that God has shown them, then they complete the vocation of ancient Israel to be "a kingdom of priests and a holy nation" (Ex. 19:6) to a needy, and watching, world. They are God's temple within a creation in rebellion against its Creator, an oasis to which

> many peoples shall come, and say,
> "Come, let us go up to the mountain of the LORD,
>   to the house of the God of Jacob,
> that he may teach us his ways
>   and that we may walk in his paths." (Isa. 2:3)

One day, when the church's work and witness are finished, God himself will restore the world's original justice, abundance, and peace, and the multitudes from all nations who have faithfully followed the Lamb will live in his presence, in this new creation, forever. This is the great hope of the follower of Jesus in the midst of life's many present difficulties. Because God is so gracious, he has not left his human creatures to wallow in the mire of their own rebellion against him. He has undertaken costly and concrete steps to put the

---

24. Baugh, *Ephesians*, 129.

world right. He has also invited his human creatures to join him in this task and in the new world it will eventually create. They do this by trusting in and following God's great king, Jesus, and by living in the power of the Holy Spirit. There is no better way to be the human being God created each of us to be.

For Further Reading

Alexander, J. A. *Commentary on the Prophecies of Isaiah.* Edited by John Eadie. 2 vols. New York: Scribner, Armstrong, 1878.

Alexander, T. Desmond. *The City of God and the Goal of Creation.* Short Studies in Biblical Theology. Wheaton, IL: Crossway, 2018.

Arnold, Clinton E. *Power and Magic: The Concept of Power in Ephesians.* Grand Rapids, MI: Baker, 1992.

Bauckham, Richard. *The Theology of the Book of Revelation.* New Testament Theology. Cambridge: Cambridge University Press, 1993.

Baugh, S. M. *Ephesians.* Evangelical Exegetical Commentary. Bellingham, WA: Lexham, 2016.

Beale, G. K. *The Book of Revelation: A Commentary on the Greek Text.* New International Greek Testament Commentary. Grand Rapids, MI: Eerdmans, 1999.

Beale, G. K. *The Temple and the Church's Mission: A Biblical Theology of the Dwelling Place of God.* New Studies in Biblical Theology 17. Downers Grove, IL: InterVarsity Press, 2004.

Block, Daniel I. *The Book of Ezekiel: Chapters 1–24.* New International Commentary on the Old Testament. Grand Rapids, MI: Eerdmans, 1997.

Block, Daniel I. *The Book of Ezekiel, Chapters 25–48.* New International Commentary on the Old Testament. Grand Rapids, MI: Eerdmans, 1998.

Bruce, F. F. *The Book of the Acts.* Rev. ed. New International Commentary on the New Testament. Grand Rapids, MI: Eerdmans, 1988.

Davies, W. D., and Dale C. Allison Jr. *The Gospel according to Saint Matthew*, International Critical Commentary. 3 vols. London: T&T Clark, 1988–1997.

Eadie, John. *Commentary on the Epistle to the Ephesians.* 3rd ed. Edinburgh: T&T Clark, 1883.

Fitzmyer, Joseph A. *The Acts of the Apostles: A New Translation with Introduction and Commentary.* Anchor Bible 31. New York: Doubleday, 1998.

Green, Peter. *Alexander to Actium: The Historical Evolution of the Hellenistic Age.* Hellenistic Culture and Society 1. Berkeley: University of California Press, 1990.

Harris, Murray J. *The Second Epistle to the Corinthians: A Commentary on the Greek Text.* New International Greek Testament Commentary. Grand Rapids, MI: Eerdmans, 2005.

Hengel, Martin. *Crucifixion in the Ancient World and the Folly of the Message of the Cross.* Translated by John Bowden. Philadelphia: Fortress, 1977.

House, Paul R. *Isaiah.* Mentor Commentary. 2 vols. Fearn, Ross-shire, Scotland: Mentor, 2019.

Hubbard, Moyer V. *New Creation in Paul's Letters and Thought.* Society for New Testament Studies Monograph Series 119. Cambridge: Cambridge University Press, 2002.

Jackson, T. Ryan. *New Creation in Paul's Letters: A Study of the Historical and Social Setting of a Pauline Concept.* Wissenschaftliche Untersuchungen zum Neuen Testament, 2nd ser., vol. 272. Tübingen: Mohr Siebeck, 2010.

Jones, Peter, and Keith Sidwell, eds. *The World of Rome: An Introduction to Roman Culture.* Cambridge: Cambridge University Press, 1997.

Keener, Craig S. *Acts: An Exegetical Commentary.* 4 vols. Grand Rapids, MI: Baker, 2012–2015.

Lincoln, Andrew T. *Ephesians*. Word Biblical Commentary 42. Dallas: Word Books, 1990.

McConville, J. G. *Deuteronomy*. Apollos Old Testament Commentary. Downers Grove, IL: InterVarsity Press, 2002.

McConville, J. G. *Grace in the End: A Study of Deuteronomic Theology*. Studies in Old Testament Biblical Theology. Grand Rapids, MI: Zondervan, 1993.

Moo, Douglas J. "Creation and New Creation." *Bulletin for Biblical Research* 20, no. 1 (2010): 39–60.

Osborne, Grant R. *Matthew*. Zondervan Exegetical Commentary on the New Testament. Grand Rapids, MI: Zondervan, 2010.

Oswalt, John N. *The Book of Isaiah, Chapters 1–39*. New International Commentary on the Old Testament. Grand Rapids, MI: Eerdmans, 1986.

Oswalt, John N. *The Book of Isaiah, Chapters 40–66*. New International Commentary on the Old Testament. Grand Rapids, MI: Eerdmans, 1998.

Plantinga, Cornelius, Jr. *Not the Way It's Supposed to Be: A Breviary of Sin*. Grand Rapids, MI: Eerdmans, 1995.

Sarna, Nahum M. *Exodus*. JPS Torah Commentary. Philadelphia: Jewish Publication Society, 1991.

Sarna, Nahum M. *Genesis*. JPS Torah Commentary. Philadelphia: Jewish Publication Society, 1989.

Stott, John R. W. *God's New Society: The Message of Ephesians*. Downers Grove, IL: InterVarsity Press, 1979.

Stuart, Douglas K. *Exodus*. New American Commentary 2. Nashville: Broadman and Holman, 2006.

Swete, Henry Barclay. *The Apocalypse of St. John*. 3rd ed. London: Macmillan, 1911.

Thielman, Frank. *Ephesians*. Baker Exegetical Commentary on the New Testament. Grand Rapids, MI: Baker Academic, 2010.

Thielman, Frank. *The Law and the New Testament: The Question of Continuity.* Companions to the New Testament. New York: Crossroad, 1999.

Thielman, Frank. *Paul and the Law: A Contextual Approach.* Downers Grove, IL: InterVarsity Press, 1994.

Thielman, Frank. *The Theology of the New Testament: A Canonical and Synthetic Approach.* Grand Rapids, MI: Zondervan, 2005.

Thompson, J. A. *The Book of Jeremiah.* New International Commentary on the Old Testament. Grand Rapids, MI: Eerdmans, 1980.

Toner, Jerry. *Popular Culture in Ancient Rome.* Cambridge: Polity, 2009.

Ware, James P. *Paul's Theology in Context: Creation, Incarnation, Covenant, and Kingdom.* Grand Rapids, MI: Eerdmans, 2019.

Wenham, Gordon J. *Genesis 1–15.* Word Biblical Commentary 1. Nashville: Thomas Nelson, 1987.

Wenham, Gordon J. *Rethinking Genesis 1–11: Gateway to the Bible.* Eugene, OR: Cascade Books, 2015.

Wright, Christopher J. H. *The Mission of God: Unlocking the Bible's Grand Narrative.* Downers Grove, IL: IVP Academic, 2006.

Wright, N. T. *The Resurrection of the Son of God.* Vol. 3 of *Christian Origins and the Question of God.* Minneapolis: Fortress, 2003.

General Index

Scripture Index

Short Studies in Biblical Theology Series

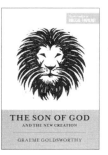

THE SON OF GOD
AND THE NEW CREATION

GRAEME GOLDSWORTHY

MARRIAGE
AND THE MYSTERY OF THE GOSPEL

RAY ORTLUND

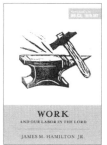

WORK
AND OUR LABOR IN THE LORD

JAMES M. HAMILTON JR.

COVENANT
AND GOD'S PURPOSE FOR THE WORLD

THOMAS R. SCHREINER

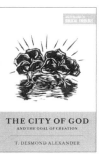

THE CITY OF GOD
AND THE GOAL OF CREATION

T. DESMOND ALEXANDER

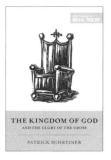

THE KINGDOM OF GOD
AND THE GLORY OF THE CROSS

PATRICK SCHREINER

FROM CHAOS TO COSMOS
CREATION TO NEW CREATION

SIDNEY GREIDANUS

THE LORD'S SUPPER
AS THE SIGN AND MEAL OF THE NEW COVENANT

GUY PRENTISS WATERS

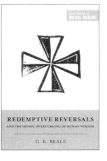

REDEMPTIVE REVERSALS
AND THE IRONIC OVERTURNING OF HUMAN WISDOM

G. K. BEALE

DIVINE BLESSING
AND THE FULLNESS OF LIFE IN THE PRESENCE OF GOD

WILLIAM R. OSBORNE

THE SERPENT
AND THE SERPENT SLAYER

ANDREW DAVID NASELLI

THE NEW CREATION
AND THE STORYLINE OF SCRIPTURE

FRANK THIELMAN

For more information, visit **crossway.org/ssbt**.